Thanks for all you do for kids! Cathi

THE CAN DO WORKPLACE

A STRENGTHS-BASED MODEL FOR NONPROFITS

CATHI CORIDAN MA

D1468729

MOtivational PRESS®
LEADERS IN GLOBAL PUBLISHING

Published by Motivational Press, Inc.
1777 Aurora Road
Melbourne, Florida, 32935
www.MotivationalPress.com

Manufactured in the United States of America.

ISBN: 978-1-62865-234-5

Contents

Foreword to the 'Can Do' Workplace

By: Michelle Kinder

Executive Director

Momentous Institute

Dallas, TX

Cathi Coridan lives, 'Can Do'. Not because things have been easy for her. Quite the opposite. Which, when you think about it, isn't surprising. It's during our most challenging times that we cannot hide from ourselves. Those times when we recognize with absolute clarity the incredible significance of our attitudes, beliefs, spirit, and assumptions.

This has certainly been true for Cathi's journey and it's true for all of us.

In addition to being consistently grounded in positivity, Cathi is driven by curiosity and it's this posture of curiosity, combined with over 40 years in organizational development, which fueled the question that led to Cathi's new book. *I know 'Can Do' made all the difference in my personal life. What does it look like when organizational culture/ climate centers around that same ethos?*

With this new book, Cathi turns her, *Can Do,* lens onto the work place -- Studying what makes the difference -- Studying why some organizations falter despite support and a strong sense of mission -- and studying why some organizations face incredible challenges and just keep thriving.

Not surprisingly, the answer to this question is complex and layered. It's as much art as it is science. But, as Cathi spent time doing deep dives with several organizations across the country, some definite themes emerged which are explored in the pages ahead.

Dr. Jill Bolte Taylor is now famous for encouraging all of us to, 'Please take responsibility for the energy you bring into this space.' There is so much out of our control. This book is about what is in our control and how we can take charge of it – fully embody a 'can-do' spirit and make a real difference for ourselves and the people around us.

INTRODUCTION

THE JOURNEY FROM CAN'T DO TO CAN DO

The nonprofit workplace: that place where over 10 million of us spend between 40 to 50, (and, often more), hours a week and where, hopefully, we make a positive difference in the world because everyone knows that people in our sector are not in it for the money! As a "seasoned nonprofit professional," my commitment is to help build and strengthen the sector I care so deeply about so that we, as mission-based organizations, can make what I call, "a Can Do kind of difference," in our little parts of the world.

One thing we all know: our work is not easy. Across all areas of the sector – from human services to health services, from advocacy groups to the arts, from education to environmental groups – the 21st century has changed our sector, first through a much more intensive focus on accountability and evidence-based outcomes, which was quickly followed by the financial wallop of the Great Recession. The nonprofit sector, as a reflection of the larger communities that we serve, remains in a state of continuous change that provides a wide range of challenges to the work we are trying to do and the impact we want to achieve.

One of the best things to happen in the last twenty years is that a diverse literature base has developed to help support our work and address the issues and needs of the growing nonprofit sector. This collection of experts provides the field with a wide variety of coaches and teachers to support us as we work and strive toward success. Some of these masters have inspired my work through the years and have helped to frame the ideas that have grown into the "Can Do Workplace" model.

For example, the late Stephen Covey understood mission like few others: after all, his second habit of highly effective people is to begin with the end in mind. And, he also understood that it is very difficult to execute on strategies to achieve goals in the midst of what he calls the "whirlwind of distractions,"[i] which are abundant in the "do more with less" nonprofit workday.

Peter Drucker understood the connection of change & growth like few others: "Everybody has accepted by now that change is unavoidable. But that still implies that change is like death and taxes — it should be postponed as long as possible and no change would be vastly preferable. But in a period of upheaval, such as the one we are living in, change is the norm."[ii]

While some writers and experts have stated that the nonprofit sector needs to become more business-like, Jim Collins, in his follow up monograph[iii] on his seminal work, "***Good to Great,***" that focuses on the nonprofit sector says it's not just about being more business-like."...we need a new language. The critical distinction is not between business and social, but between great and good. We need to reject the naïve imposition of the 'language of business' on the social sectors, and instead jointly embrace a *language of greatness.*[iv] He focuses on achieving greatness by building a culture of discipline. A culture of discipline is not a principle of business; it is a principle of greatness."

It is in the same spirit of the authors of these works that I present the "Can Do Workplace" model. I don't for a minute believe that I have the same level of understanding of business and management systems that these great teachers possess, but what I do bring is over 40 years of experience in the nonprofit, education, and human services fields that I am constantly working to combine with the wisdom I have garnered from these giants' work. I have filled numerous roles as line staff, program manager, department director, CEO, consultant, and Board member in numerous nonprofits. These positions and experiences have provided me the opportunity to garner and build upon hundreds of lessons learned, both good and bad; and, when I can, to share those lessons. My experiences range from great successes, to periods of extreme struggle, and sometimes just plain surviving. Combining my experiences with the input and ideas of teachers, mentors, coaches, colleagues and friends, I present the "Can Do Workplace" model as one more tool in the tool belt for managers and leaders to use as they work to produce the dynamic mission-based outcomes that each of us, who work hard in this sector, give so much of ourselves to achieve.

If I had to boil the "Can Do" model down to one summary sentence, I would use this one that learned from Momentous Institute, and which was echoed over and over again throughout the interview, research, and writing process: *it all starts with connected relationships.*

The "Can't Do" Workplaces.

Before I begin to unpack, define, and describe the "Can Do Workplace" model, I want to explore how is it that many nonprofit organizations seem to get, and stay, stuck in the muck and mire of "*Can't Do*", where the leaders and employees want to meet their goals and provide great service and excellent products, yet things don't turn out the way they planned. These are good, dedicated people trying so hard to do the right thing, yet they are achieving uneven, little, or no success.

I have worked in and with nonprofits as a program manager, director, CEO, and consultant where I have watched, listened, and participated as organizations get stuck and then struggle to try to get un-stuck, missing their outcome goals again and again. Some establish goals and set expectations that are unrealistic, without the strategies, resources, or capacity to meet them, then find themselves with predictable product or service outcomes and accompanying negative employee and client attitudes – and yet they are surprised! Sometimes, the focus gets stuck on the negative forces at play, i.e., the non-responsive economy and lingering impact of the recession, lack of revenue, poor employee performance, positions that had to get cut, what cannot get done, who's to blame... So, over and over again these leaders revise the language, reword the goals and reorganize the teams, set up a new plan; but the outcomes are the same. That is when their people, (read: employees, clients and funders), become frustrated and leave.

In nonprofit organizations with a *"Can't Do"* culture, morale suffers, people become disengaged, quit trying or just plain quit, and bad outcomes and worst case scenarios become a reality. The cycle repeats and the experiences snowball... It is painful to watch, and excruciating to experience – as an employee, as a client, or as a customer.

I have encountered another kind of *"Can't Do"* workplace more than once along my career path. It is an organization that looks good and appears to function well and be very successful on the outside, but suffers from serious neglect of its core infrastructure, i.e., employee professional development, financial management, accounting and reporting, contract compliance requirements, employee evaluation, conflict of interest, etc. I have been told by nonprofit Boards that some critical mission-based changes were "non-negotiable," and informed by some program managers in the face of losing their jobs that they "just cannot change." The result is an erosion that creates a series of sink holes, putting the organization at risk, or even out of business, much to the surprise of funders, clients, and the community it serves.

As a consultant, I have tried to counsel senior managers when employees have desperately needed tools and guidance that were vaguely promised, but never delivered. It is painful to watch the revolving door as staff leaves and outcome goals are never quite met. As an Interim CEO, I have had to close an organization down, with the sad knowledge that its failure and demise were totally preventable. Witnessing so many instances of unnecessary and preventable pain and failure is part of what motivated me to write this book.

▌ Changes in the Nonprofit Sector:

Most of my work has been with small to mid-sized nonprofits, so I have closely followed the nonprofit trends, changes and challenges that started in the late 1990s, beginning with the transition into new levels of accountability for outcomes and results. Then the Great Recession hit, and the majority of nonprofit organizations lost funding from most or all of their sources: individual donors, program fees, foundations, and investments. Staff positions, hours, and benefits were cut, skewering morale. At the same time, and in large part because of the Recession, the competition for both program services and program dollars reached record levels, stretching staff and resources dangerously thin. While the last few years have brought a more solid footing to the economy, many nonprofits still remain uneven and unsteady, leading me to actively wonder what makes the difference between organizations that "get it" and effectively build capacity and become resilient even in tough times, and those that struggle so hard, yet don't seem to be able to cross the thresholds to stability, sustainability and success.

▌ A Transition of Perspective:

Until recently, I feared that most nonprofits were doomed to a life-cycle of struggle and stress because that was most of what I saw in my work. In the last few years, I have come to realize that most of my belief, though not all of it, was a product of my experience and my perspective. Once my perspective changed, everything changed!

Also, I am humbled to confess that I, myself, have contributed to the "Can't Do" culture in some instances. Sometimes it was by jumping on the negativity wagon, looking for and magnifying what was wrong. Or, I was working to remedy systemic issues with a defensive chip on my shoulder, so while I was fighting for the right, I did so with a whine in my voice that clouded my message and impeded my progress. At one point, I had righteous indignation down to a fine art which, in retrospect, was a huge waste of my talent and my time. I share some of those experiences in Chapter 5. But, now that my perspective has changed, I can state with firm conviction that I will not go back to those approaches.

My "Can Do Life" started when I made a decision - during one of my life's most stressful moments, on June 18, 2010 when my husband's job was eliminated just after I resigned my nonprofit CEO position for health reasons - to focus on the possibilities and be grateful for the resources at hand. In late 2013, I wrote and published my first book, "*The Can Do Chronicles*", where I share my personal story of being transformed during a three year period of painful and unrelenting financial, work, and health challenges, punctuated by undergoing six (successful!) months of chemo. That critical life transformation took me from someone with a perennial chip on my shoulder to someone who lives my life grounded in gratitude, yet based in reality. As my "Can Do" world view gained traction and took on a life of its own, it become far too important to me to risk losing it. Because I believe in the power of stories to teach and motivate, I wrote the first book to share my story and the potential and promise of living a "Can Do Life". Once I got healthy, I began to consider how the concepts and practices I had developed and described on a personal level could be applied on an organizational level to help and support nonprofits to become more successful, more Can Do. So, I set about to write the "Can Do Workplace".

▌ The Evolution of the "Can Do Workplace":

The process of writing this book was not as easy as I first imagined. I began by revisiting key organizational concepts from my training and experience in the nonprofit sector; then I dove into the literature and engaged in several dozen fascinating interviews with nonprofit leaders from across the country and around the world. With a simple posting on Linked In, I met leaders from over a dozen organizations that are fully invested in the "Can Do" approach to their nonprofit work, whether they had called it that or not. It was refreshing and very inspiring. Then, I called upon colleagues whom I knew were committed to the "Can Do" model to further unpack and more deeply explore their practices and organizational cultures with me. The process was inspiring and so filled with hope!

Slowly, I developed, tested, and refined my working definition, organizing concepts and core practices of a "Can Do Workplace". Weeks turned into months of talking, reading, and writing, and just when I would think I had defined the formula, or captured the right combination of practices and concepts, I would hear or glean a new element, a new dimension from a conversation, an article, or through the process of writing, and want to develop and find ways to incorporate it into the "Can Do Workplace" model.

These ideas and concepts include the Social Emotional Health model that is the core operating concept at the Momentous Institute; learning organizations made famous by Dr. Peter Senge in the 1990s; strengths-based leadership which is at the core of the Environmental Leadership Program; and, the emerging work of Dr. Carol Dweck on the Growth Mindset. I found, bought, and marked up books and articles on gratitude in the workplace, and how it is contributing to making change with quality and wholistic approaches to effective nonprofit management. The "Can Do" model, while simple, has a network of connections to other critical works. So I revisited the concepts, ideas, and approaches I had learned through the years from Stephen Covey, most notably the Four Disciplines of Execution; Jim Collins' Good To Great for the Social Sector; and the ageless foundational work of Peter Drucker and John W. Gardner. And, finally, took out my books and articles from my Nonprofit Executive Management Certificate program to revisit the core concepts and challenges of the larger nonprofit sector.

With all of this excellent material already available, I had to ask myself the very difficult question of whether "Can Do" is distinct enough from all of these, from the other emerging works and from the masters whom I have studied for years. "Yes, why yes it is," I concluded. "Can Do" is an innovative and important approach – not the only important one, but one that works together with the others to strengthen and move the nonprofit sector forward, one organization at a time.

There are hundreds of struggling nonprofits out there; I see them and hear about them every day. This book is designed to provide their leaders and managers with models and concepts, along with fresh ideas and guidance for implementing strategies and practices. Unlike some resources, it provides a clear and well-defined place to start. "Can Do" cannot be based on maybes or wishes or hopes; and, certainly not just on a quick reframing that essentially repeats the past with slight changes. The "Can Do" model starts, as it did for me and for the people who have been most successful, with a strong, unyielding commitment to mission, a pervasive culture of gratitude, and a resolute focus on achieving growth by identifying and moving toward realistic possibilities – every. single. day.

Those leaders and managers for whom "Can Do" has been successful have kept their promise to take the "but..." out of "yes, but..." and to lose the excuses and fully commit to and focus on what they CAN DO. They still encounter challenges and make, (and admit and then learn from), mistakes. They are not awarded every grant and not every project goes to scale. They understand these challenges are the realities and cost of doing business and don't let such things get in their way. Rather, they look for new ways to make decisions and solve problems, repeatedly asking themselves and everyone else, "What else can we do?"

Do you want your nonprofit and the people you serve to be more successful? Do you want the outcomes of your programs and services to make real, meaningful and lasting impact for your clients, your employees and your community? Do you want to reduce workplace stress and increase productivity? If your answers are YES, then this book is for you! Even if your answers are currently YES, BUT… this book is still for you.

And, if you are lucky like I was, you might learn not just how the "Can Do" model can transform your workplace; the "Can Do" model just might change your life!

About This Book

The "Can Do Workplace" is a guide for nonprofit leaders and managers to engage in discussions, brainstorming, planning, and executing plans to sustain and strengthen their employees, their services, and the people and communities that they serve.

A Nonprofit Focus:

When I began the "Can Do Workplace" project, I intended to research and write about how the "Can Do Workplace" model would benefit nonprofit agencies and small businesses. Early on, I made the decision to focus only on the nonprofit sector. Part of the decision is personal because it is my home sector, where I have served as manager and CEO, Board member, earned an executive certificate, provided coaching and consultation to dozens of staff and CEOs. I have developed case statements for support and authored hundreds of grant proposals that have secured millions of dollars to support great missions.

But, there is more than my personal commitment to the sector that drives my decision to focus this book on nonprofits. It is the role that nonprofit organizations and staff play, the work that they do, and the passion and compassion of the leaders, managers, staff and volunteers. I greatly admire and am grateful for the difference that our nonprofits make in all of our lives, but primarily in the lives of the people that they serve. The people who, without the nonprofits, would have many fewer options and much less quality in any options available.

I want the nonprofits to become more "Can Do" so that their stories can be told; so that the quality of programs increase and the funding streams continue to grow. So that an elderly woman in Atlanta doesn't have to eat cat food at the end of the month anymore. So that middle school girls in underserved neighborhoods in DC and Dallas can meet their goals of being the first in their families to attend college. So that the families who are homeless in Worcester can stay together at a shelter that provides them hospitality and hope. And the list goes on.

A Look Ahead at the Rest of the Book

Use of Case Stories:

From my interviews with dozens people in organizations around the world, I selected four diverse nonprofit organizations to feature as "case stories" that illustrate the "Can Do" model, with each bringing a specific practice of the "Can Do" model to life in a dynamic and unique way. The more I learned about their missions and approach to work, the more I wanted to introduce you to them, and let you learn more about this group of extraordinary nonprofit organizations – their missions, their impact, and their truly remarkable people. In order to maximize the power of the stories of these four amazing organizations and their people to animate the "Can Do Workplace" elements, I decided to locate these insightful "case stories" at the heart of the book instead of taking them on as "case studies" in the appendix.

Because this is a book about workplaces, the case stories focus more on the staff and working conditions than on the people served. Within each of the case stories, I introduce their distinctive "Can Do" approaches and workplace cultures, and highlight the lasting impact that they have on their work, their people, and their communities. I encourage you, the reader, to dig deeper and to learn more about the four organizations - visit their websites, Google their leaders, read the stories that they share. Let their work and stories inspire and motivate you and your staff to find out what more you Can Do!

Lessons-Learned Case Studies:

In Chapter 5, four short case studies provide a counter point to the case stories with lessons I have learned as a nonprofit leader. Each of them comes from my employment or consulting experience, and relates one of the four core practices of a "Can Do Workplace" model. Several of these case studies were painfully difficult to write, but once completed, very freeing. From this experience, I recommend all nonprofit leaders take the time and use them as a model to examine and then write about their own critical lessons learned.

Approach:

The "Can Do Workplace" is being written not just as a book to read and put on the shelf, but a book to use again and again with managers and leadership teams. Throughout the book, I combine and connect the "Can Do" model with emerging and established leadership and management models and approaches from the literature; and then I try to add some common sense and conventional wisdom. Because I think that sometimes we try too hard to be profound and miss out on the obvious, I try to keep the approaches and suggested activities practical and the language in the book straightforward and as free of jargon as possible. I recommend digging deeper into the books and authors I include in Chapter 8 and use these resources to work on some of the activities recommended in Chapter 7. Not every element in this book will fit every nonprofit organization out there. That said, where you feel resistance, I fully recommend you dig deeper to find out why before letting it go.

So, whether you are a leader or manager in an organization that:

» "Can't quite do" and whose leaders already know they need to make a changes.

» One that is stumbling and trying to succeed, but with confused, or possibly clueless, leadership.

» Or one that is seriously struggling and looking for effective strategies to restructure to move forward differently and more effectively.

I hope you find that this book provides an effective starting point.

Read on. Use the case concepts, case stories, case studies, and the strategies and activities in Chapter 7 to:

» engage your employees on all levels

» improve communication

» strengthen decision making

» focus on meeting your clients' needs through your mission, and

» begin to make a "Can Do" difference in your little corner of the world

I wish you great success, much learning and many insights on your journey.

CHAPTER 1

THE "CAN DO WORKPLACE": A STRENGTHS-BASED MODEL FOR NONPROFITS

❙ Let's Start With the "Can Do Workplace" Definition:

An intentional work environment that encourages, promotes, and supports system-wide and individual employee excellence for change & growth. It is where meeting the needs of the people being served, with excellence, is at the heart of the work every day. And, it is a place where strategic change, mission-inspired growth, and a persistent attitude of gratitude are the expectation and the norm.

It is where

CAN = what is possible

Meets DO = the action to make it real

"Can Do" is a life element within an organization that both defines it and naturally elevates it above its peers, both in terms of excellence as a great place to work and also as a high impact and successful organization that makes a difference in its community. These two aspects are inseparable.

Can Do Workplace Practices:

To help me quantify and effectively describe the core elements and determinants of a "Can Do Workplace", I engaged in dozens of fascinating conversations with nonprofit leaders, board members, CEOs, volunteers, and managers from around the world. Even as I finish my writing, I continue to dig deeper, returning to my notes, and transcriptions from those insightful and dynamic dialogues to discover what the common practices and elements are that move an organization from being "good" or "very good" up and into the "Can Do" category.

I have narrowed "Can Do Workplace" elements down to four core practices that define ways that people at all levels in organizations:

1) Align their goals and activities to achieve mission all the way through the organization;

2) Make decisions based on possibilities and accountability;

3) Predict and manage change for growth; and finally,

4) Formulate and simmer their "secret sauce."

Alignment, decision-making, managing change, & growth and the quality of the secret sauce. Several other practices emerged time and again to support those four, such as how well they communicate across systems, turn mistakes into lessons learned, turn threats into opportunities, deal with ambiguous situations, and strategically invest in the future and continued success. But the core four remain as the strong, enduring framework.

At its core, the "Can Do" aspects of an organization – both those about its services and products and those about its employees – involve aligning, believing in and working to intentionally combine mission, vision, and values for everyone, every day. "Can Do" is what makes an organization - a workplace - special and unique. You know it when it's there, and you know when it is not.

"Can Do" can be an elusive quality or concept to wrap our heads around. It is about the organizational culture and the quality of the organization's impact, yet there is more. Its four component framework is built upon a solid foundation consisting of two critical elements:

1. A well-defined, meaningful mission that drives all of its activities, and

2. An organizational culture that is grounded in gratitude.

The outcome is awesome! Everyone in a "Can Do" organization understands and appreciates that what they do makes a positive difference for both the people being served and the people doing the serving. While it can sound a little like nirvana to work there, the "Can Do Workplace" remains solidly grounded in reality where employees encounter and deal effectively with real, hard problems, make mistakes, and learn from them. "Can Do" is messy and not perfect, but committed to working toward excellence every day. At some point, the people working in "Can Do" organizations reach the moment when they recognize and believe that the work they are doing is the "critical asset moving the needle," and that their work will be leveraged, (or defeated), by quality of belief and attitudes of the people doing that work. It does not get much better than this!

It all starts with connected relationships. Impact is achieved when the organization continues to call out the best in everyone and to work hard, with excellence, as the needle keeps moving, and then moves more. The "Can Do" quality emerges from inside the culture and guts of the organization; it cannot be added on. Once the "Can Do" level of operating is achieved, it becomes too important to the people in, and those served by, the organization to lose it. It takes time, commitment, persistent effort, without shortcuts and must be sustained. But, it is absolutely worth it!

"Can Do" leaders know that they are not invincible; they remain aware that there are some "cancers" that can, and will, kill "Can Do". Without a commitment to mission and a culture grounded in gratitude, the practices alone will not achieve the "Can Do" level of difference. All the "timely tips" and "5 steps to a better…" in the world won't work without gratitude and focus on mission. When the foundation, (mission & gratitude), and the framework, (four core practices), are combined, the "Can Do" qualities emerge as a gestalt = much more than the sum of all of the parts.

A word of caution:

There's NOT an app for "Can Do"! "Can Do Workplaces" cannot be designed in one meeting, or built strong in a month. There are no silver bullets, hacks, or easy fixes that transform struggling, okay, or even good organizations into "Can Do Workplaces". The successful "Can Do" model is iterative, long term, difficult, and messy. It is up to the leaders to engage, inspire, invest in, and then leverage the commitment of the people in their organization and to employ the ideas and concepts in the model to create, execute, and sustain their own, customized "Can Do Workplace". Shortcuts and half-steps create sink holes in an organization that require much more energy to repair than doing it right in the first place requires to achieve excellence. As they say at Momentous Institute, "We work hard & that is good."

CHAPTER 2

WHAT MAKES A "CAN DO WORKPLACE" WORK?

▌The Foundation: Mission & Gratitude

Before we get started discussing the practices and implementation of the "Can Do Workplace", there are two critical elements that are foundational, so primary that they come before the others.

These critical elements are:

1. A well-defined, meaningful mission that drives all of its activities, and

2. An organizational culture that is grounded in gratitude.

I believe that any nonprofit organization without these elements will have a very difficult, if not impossible, time mastering and successfully implementing the practices of the "Can Do Workplace" model.

Mission and gratitude are easy to talk about, but difficult to fully achieve; and, once achieved, they require continuous attention to be

The Can Do Workplace

Mission & Gratitude

maintained. Together, they form a protective membrane that helps move the organization forward, protects against negative influences and blends just the right ingredients into the organization's secret sauce!

Mission:

All nonprofit organizations have an identified mission and a mission statement that defines their reason for being. What sets a "Can Do Workplace" apart is that its mission is:

» The central organizing element of the organization = is too important to get lost in the busy-ness or challenges of the work day and its deliverables.

» Well-defined = able to be understood by clients and by the highest and lowest paid employees.

» Meaningful = adds positive value to the lives of the people it serves and treats everyone with respect and dignity.

» Unifying = connected to and drives all activities, from the reception desk to the business office, to the program delivery to the Board room and beyond.

Your mission is your most valuable asset. Let me repeat. Most. Valuable. Asset. More valuable than your building, than your financial reserves, than your volunteers, and, yes, more valuable than your staff. Really? Yes. Because the mission is why the board and staff show up. The mission is why the building was built, why the reserves are in place, why you have a good reputation in the community. Your mission is the "why" of your organization. Brinckerhoff, Peter C. Smart Stewardship for Nonprofits: Making the Right Decision in Good Times and Bad. Wiley, NY: 2012

The mission is the core of the organization, its legal reason for existence, but goes much further than that. All of the work of the organization and the people who do that work must draw motivation from and be focused on achieving the mission every day. Not just before a board meeting, fund raising campaign, or accreditation site visit. Every day.

I believe that nonprofits are exceptionally fortunate to have their mission as the core motivator. In the business and corporate worlds, where the focus is more on profit and margin, it requires a very different kind of energy and effort to inspire and motivate the workforce. Nonprofits have mission.

> *"A 'Can Do Workplace' has a good mission, then a commitment to pursue that mission in everything it does." -Yasmina Vinci, Executive Director of the National Head Start Association, Alexandria, VA*

An organization that wants to transform to be a "Can Do Workplace" needs to revisit and review its mission and ask:

- » How well defined is it?
- » How dated is it? How relevant is it today?
- » Does everyone in the organization know the mission? How well can they describe it to others? Are there environmental cues that reflect and reinforce the mission?
- » How does the mission influence how decisions are made across the organization?
- » How does the mission strengthen and build the community that the organization serves?

Gratitude:

Almost as if it is part of the oxygen in the atmosphere, a "Can Do Workplace" has an integrated and ingrained organizational culture that is grounded in gratitude, evidenced in formal and informal interactions and communication, from customer care and service to employee compensation and recognition. Together with mission, a culture of gratitude forms a solid foundation to contain, nurture and sustain the "Can Do Workplace". It starts at the top and goes all the way through; it is practiced consistently; and it is genuine. This attitude of gratitude is equally evident when things are going well and when crisis or problems arise. In fact, having a strong culture of gratitude helps organizations weather crisis and emerge stronger as a result.

There is an emerging science and neuroscience of gratitude. Robert Emmons' work has begun to explore the power that gratitude has to transform and reward. According to Emmons, "gratitude has one of the strongest links to mental health and satisfaction with life of any personality trait—more so than even optimism, hope, or compassion. Gratitude is important not only because it helps us feel good but also because it inspires us to do good. Gratitude heals, energizes, and transforms lives in myriad ways consistent with the notion that virtue is its own reward and produces other rewards."[v] Where better than the workplace, where we spend such a big percentage of our time, to have and practice gratitude?

Yet, the workplace is the one place that many people find it hardest to express gratitude. That may be what makes working in a "Can Do Workplace" so pleasantly different; it is a workplace where gratitude is an expectation and is widely practiced all the way through the organization.

In an article published on the website of the Greater Good Science Center at the University of California at Berkeley, author and editor Jeremy Adam Smith notes, "Elsewhere in American life, we say "thank you" to acknowledge the good things we get from other people, especially when they give out of the goodness of their hearts. We say "thanks" at home and in school, in stores, and at church. But not at work. According to a survey of 2,000 Americans released in early 2013 by the John Templeton

Foundation, people are less likely to feel or express gratitude at work than anyplace else. And they're not thankful for their current jobs, ranking them dead last in a list of things they're grateful for."[vi]

All of us have heard the traditional arguments and questions, "Why should we thank someone for doing the work that we are paying them to do?" "I thank them every two weeks with their paycheck." And, implying it is thankless: "This is why they call it work!"

The critical thing to remember about gratitude is the power it has to change people and their experience of situations. Gratitude helps focus on the good outcomes, not ignoring the challenges and not-so-good outcomes, but also not dwelling on them. Gratitude helps build stronger relationships among co-workers, who can then feel more comfortable to work off each other's strengths and be more effective, efficient and productive. Yet, according to the Templeton Foundation study, while almost all respondents reported that saying "thank you" to colleagues "makes me feel happier and more fulfilled"— on a given day, only 10 percent acted on that impulse. A stunning 60 percent said they "either never express gratitude at work or do so perhaps once a year." In short, Americans actively suppress gratitude on the job, even to the point of robbing themselves of happiness.[vii]

According to Emmons, gratitude as an embedded culture in the workplace can help people prepare for and come through crisis more intact. Cultivating a culture of gratitude might be the best way to help a workplace prepare for stresses that come with change, conflict, and failure. Making gratitude a core value and a practice "builds up a sort of psychological immune system that can cushion us when we fall. There is scientific evidence that grateful people are more resilient to stress, whether minor everyday hassles or major personal upheavals."[viii]

While the research and the daily experience clearly demonstrates that building a culture of gratitude at work is not easy, the science and daily experience also says it's worth it. Gratitude is the hallmark and what brings promise in and to a "Can Do Workplace". Without gratitude, you are left with a "Maybe Do" or "Make Do" Workplace, and those are just not the same.

The Four Practices of the Can Do Model:

Mission and gratitude form the foundation. The framework or backbone of a "Can Do Workplace" is built through consistent adherence to its four defining practices:

1.   FULL ALIGNMENT: A "Can Do Workplace" establishes and maintains alignment of the organization's values and its work to its mission and services delivered, and it promotes and ensures adequate communication and consistent accountability to support the mission. This alignment runs from the top to the bottom of the organization as well as laterally. All of work done in an organization is connected to the mission, whether it is the work of the CEO, the receptionist, the line staff, the maintenance staff, or the accountant.

Alignment ensures that mission runs all the way through the organization, and is so central that everyone in the organization can answer the "Why?" question with clarity and consistency. Boundaries are well established in a "Can Do Workplace" so that everyone knows what they are responsible for and how it contributes to the mission and outcomes for the people being served.

Strong alignment connects the What = Mission with the How = Implementation and Delivery and helps to ensure that resources, knowledge, and accountability are incorporated into all program delivery or services.

Priorities are established and modified as necessary. Information about changes and adjustments to forecasts, products, and programs is shared as soon as possible and as widely as needed and appropriate. There are effective and efficient communication systems in place so that where there is a gap, it is quickly identified and filled.

Alignment allows access across systems and up and down the organizational chart to work together, with many dotted lines and lots of cross-training and redundancy. Strong and clear alignment fosters a culture with healthy boundaries and full accountability.

With strong alignment, there is also a system of redundancy and back up. While all people are considered important and valuable, no one person is considered indispensable. This allows people to be moved within the organization in ways that are strategic and responsive to organizational or client needs.

On Alignment: "*Good intentions don't work if it does not truly line up with what folks on the front line have to do; it has to work with clear communication from the middle to the top and also back and forth.*"- Lorna Little, Executive Director, St. Agnes Home, West Hartford, CT

Alignment is the first and primary practice because without it, the rest of the practices will fall short. Alignment breaks down silos – silos that limit power, communication, and resources. Alignment helps prevents fragmenting and unnecessary duplication of efforts that lead to inefficiency and discouragement.

2. **EVERYONE MAKES QUALITY DECISIONS:** In a "Can Do Workplace", the "decision making pyramid" approach is used, where the fewest – the most risk-exposed – decisions are made at the top and the rest of the decisions should be made at the point of service delivery, using the policy decisions from the top as guidelines and boundaries. Good decisions are able to be made at all levels of the organization because there are well-defined boundaries, sufficient resources and accountability. This type of decision-making system requires strong policies that are consistently reviewed, revised, and communicated; sufficient training, along with adequate resources available to decision-makers; and back-up systems to quickly identify and correct mistakes and errors. This type of decision-making also promotes stronger employee engagement.

In a *"Can Do Workplace"*, it all starts with connected relationships, and the way it grows and sustains is with those connected relationships, so employee engagement is one of the most critical elements for success. According to the Gallup Report, *State of the American Workplace: Employee Engagement Insights for U.S. Business Leaders*, engaged workers are the lifeblood of their organizations. Gallup defines "engaged" employees as those who are involved in, enthusiastic about, and committed to their work and contribute to their organization in a positive manner.[ix] Two of the key findings of this report are:

» Although certain policies such as hours worked, flextime, and vacation time do relate to employee wellbeing, engagement levels in the work environment eclipse corporate policies.

» Work units in the top 25% of Gallup's Q12 Client Database, which measures employees' emotional engagement which ties directly to their level of discretionary effort, have significantly higher productivity, profitability, and customer ratings, less turnover and absenteeism, and fewer safety incidents than those in the bottom 25%.[x]

The quality of its decisions is what powers the organization and determines its overall health. Allowing decision making to occur at all levels of the organization is not as scary as it sounds! The key is to give the people making the decisions the resources that they need: the authority, support, and very clear boundaries; strong, well-crafted policies that are known and followed in all parts of the organization; access to all relevant information and supports; and the training and professional development required to make solid, good decisions. Expectations must be well defined and include the consequences for poor decisions, errors, and mistakes. Everyone making decisions needs to receive consistent feedback and be held accountable, which also helps to keep the focus on the best outcomes for everyone. And, it keeps everyone connected in a meaningful way to the mission of the organization.

People who are empowered to make decisions and who are given the resources that they need to do so effectively are the ones who build and maintain "Can Do Workplaces". They feel engaged, supported, and motivated to succeed. These are people who can "do it right or make it right," and know the boundaries and how far they can push to try to make it even better.

On Decision-Making: "Our decision-making is as flat as possible. We listen and let the people serve as our resource. This calls out their potential and inherent gifts."- Michael Shafer,

Director, Warm Hearts Worldwide, Chiang Mai Province, Thailand [xi]

People working in a "Can Do Workplace" do not feel threatened by the possibility of making mistakes. And, if they do make mistakes, they own them quickly and then harvest and share lessons learned with their bosses, peers and staff. As Thomas Alva Edison said, "I have not failed. I've just found 10,000 ways that won't work." The "Can Do Questions", described in detail below, provide an excellent tool for high quality decision making, combining the possibilities with realities of a situation.

More on Decision-Making: "How can I expect my staff to encourage and support the people we serve to make effective decisions if I don't provide them with the opportunity to do so themselves?"- Candida Flores, Executive Director, Family Life Education, Hartford, CT [xii]

3. **USING CHANGE TO ACHIEVE GROWTH:** The juncture of change & growth is at the heart of the "Can Do Workplace" because it is where the possibilities, power & promise of greatness and excellence reside and come to life. In the fast-paced, technology-driven world of business and nonprofit services, change is the biggest constant and it is also the primary pathway to growth. The great management guru, Peter Drucker reminds us: *the greatest danger in times of turbulence is not the turbulence – it is to act with yesterday's logic.* "Can Do Workplaces" are always prepared, ready to change, & grow. They take yesterday's lessons and combine them with tomorrow's potential; they stay alert and fresh, are nimble and can stretch.

Change & growth can be intimidating, threatening, and very hard for some people, and they put great effort into resisting it. Recently, there was a cartoon that circulated on the Internet. A speaker asks an auditorium full of people, "How many people want things to change?" All hands go up. The speaker follows that with a second question, "How many people want to make a change?" No hands up. It's a reminder. But it is also a warning!

> *"The pain comes from falling in love with your status quo and living in fear of making another choice, a choice that might not work. You might have been right then, but now isn't then, it's now." Seth Godin – daily blog June 22, 2015* [xiii]

Change is going to happen – every day – whether we like it or not. Leadership expert John W. Gardner understands that healthy leadership is about recognizing the constancy of, and making a commitment to renewal. In his seminal work, "On Leadership", he reminds us that "leaders must understand the interweaving of continuity and change."[xiv] So, while many fear change and try to hide from it, "Can Do Workplaces" put value in anticipating it, planning for it, managing it, and learning from it.

How one sees the world influences how they handle change. In 2006, Stanford psychologist Carol Dweck introduced the concepts of fixed and growth mindsets. "This growth mindset is based on the belief that your basic qualities are things you can cultivate through your efforts. Although people may differ in every which way – in their initial talents and aptitudes, interests, or temperaments – everyone can change and grow through application and experience. The growth mindset allows people to value what they're doing regardless of the outcome. They're tackling problems, charting new courses, working on important issues. Maybe they haven't found the cure for cancer, but the search was deeply meaningful."[xv]

People who work best in "Can Do Workplaces", from CEOs to line staff, have growth mindsets.

The "Can Do Workplace" model is focused on the confluence of Change & Growth, that growth spot of energy that invites innovation and pairs it with quality. Competition for the nonprofit dollars, whether through fee payment for products and services or through private and corporate philanthropy is based on how well an organization is able to demonstrate both innovation & impact. The growth mindset is what allows people to see potential and what fuels successful change for innovation & impact. It provides the commitment and stamina to go for the long haul, not just the short term payoffs. According to Dweck, "The passion for stretching yourself and sticking to it, even (or especially) when it's not going well, is the hallmark of the growth mindset. This is the mindset that allows people to thrive during some of the most challenging times in their lives."[xvi]

"Can Do Workplaces" are what Peter Senge calls learning organizations that stay on top of best practices and emerging trends in research and quality. According to Senge, learning organizations are: "…organizations where people continually expand their capacity to create the results they truly desire, where new and expansive patterns of thinking are nurtured, where collective aspiration is set free, and where people are continually learning to see the whole together."[xvii]

Growth in the "Can Do" model is always for the long term. Another great quote from Peter Drucker reminds us that, "long-range planning does not deal with future decisions, but with the future of present decisions. If you want something new, you have to stop doing something old."[xviii] It means knowing "when to say when" and choosing opportunities wisely, based on the capacity of today and the potential of tomorrow.

Not all growth is equal or healthy. Not all change leads to growth and not all change is good! Simply making plans for change and setting expectations without giving people the means to plan, prepare for, and then achieve them is a recipe for disaster. Change for the sake of or for the thrill of change, or to simply change the order or appearance of the same elements to look different are equally unhealthy and dangerous.

One critical distinction is that for "Can Do Workplaces", growth does not mean bigger. Growth could mean becoming smaller and more focused, such as creating boutique or niche programs. In the next chapter, the story of the Environmental Leadership Program provides a great illustration of an organization that grew as it reduced, restructured, and resized. And, it is thriving.

"Can Do Workplaces" employ long term goal setting combined with measured, short term objectives and well-defined steps to achieve those goals. Stephen Covey, in **The Four Disciplines of Execution** talks about WIGs, or Wildly Important Goals, that help define and focus the actions of an organization. Jim Collins talks about the BHAGs or Big Hairy Audacious Goals in much the same way. The WIGs and BHAGs are tied to vision, and enable and motivate people throughout the organization to achieve that vision. In the "Can Do Workplace", the planning and executing of the big goals is done incrementally, with well-defined short term objectives to achieve the hoped-for change and that are tracked to a timeline which is shared throughout the organization on scoreboards, in reports and in meetings.

The literature is filled with excellent resources available for making small, measured change that focuses on quality and excellence. The Breakthrough Series Model (BTS) from the Institute for Healthcare Improvement's Collaborative Model for Achieving Breakthrough Improvement[xix] is one such model. Developed within the healthcare industry, the Plan/Do/Study/Act change cycle provides a platform for testing innovations during short intervals, studying the outcomes, and making incremental, quality-driven change (or not) informed by those outcomes. Then the process repeats. Based on the concept that research is well ahead of practice, or, "we know a lot more than what our practice suggests," the BTS has been very successful in reducing errors in operating rooms and strengthening health care policies to reduce infant mortality. P/D/S/A is a model that can be readily adapted for a team or organization to use for a strategic plan implementation or as part of a program restructuring.

4.   CRAFTING AND SIMMERING THE BEST SECRET SAUCE: The Secret Sauce in a "Can Do Workplace" is the signature quality of the organization that makes its culture special and sets it apart from other places to work. It is the "je ne sais quoi" that attracts good people to and keeps them in an organization. The Secret Sauce motivates and rewards people for going above and beyond; to contribute to the greater good of each other and the organization. The Secret Sauce encourages collaboration and promotes synergy among a variety of people for richer, more complex and meaningful outcomes and impact.

Every organization has a secret sauce. Its ingredients include a combination of its corporate values, relationships, practices, people, and energy that create its signature feel and culture. The secret sauce touches employees, volunteers, Board members, and clients on an emotional level and influences an organization's reputation and position in the community. The secret sauce also amplifies the mission and is what makes an organization become a part of peoples' lives beyond the workday, volunteer event, or reception of services. When you ask donors to give because investing in your mission meets their philanthropic needs, what you are really talking about is sharing your secret sauce with them, and to keep those donors coming back with bigger and bigger checks, what is in the sauce needs to be the real thing.

Not all secret sauce is good. Things that are trying to be hidden "come out in the wash" in the sauce; and gaps and unmet needs leave an unpleasant aftertaste. People know when the sauce "comes from a bottle" versus when it genuinely emerges from the values and commitment to mission and greatness. When people leave because "it just doesn't feel right" or "the bad vibe", they are referring to the secret sauce.

As important as the ingredients are to the blend, so is intentionality in creating THE BEST secret sauce; and, not just from the leadership, though that is a must, but throughout the organization. "Good" secret sauce is just not good enough. "Can Do Workplaces" strive for THE BEST in their secret sauce, and that means constant attention is paid to the recipe and the best people are put in charge of keeping it that way. There is an extra level of engagement from staff when that intentionality to ensure that the sauce is THE BEST is there, and an increasing risk for disengagement when not. The leaders ensure that any new people will add to, not detract from the greatness of the secret sauce with their values and level of engagement and commitment to mission.

One last tip about the secret sauce recipe: Even THE BEST Secret Sauce can, and will, sour. Once an organization's secret sauce recipe is blended, simmered, and spiced to just the way they like it, to stay fresh, new ingredients need to be added – and old ingredients need to be removed – very carefully. Continuous communication and feedback about the quality and experience of the sauces needs to be gathered from internal and external sources, to prevent an unexpected, possibly bitter change to the taste.

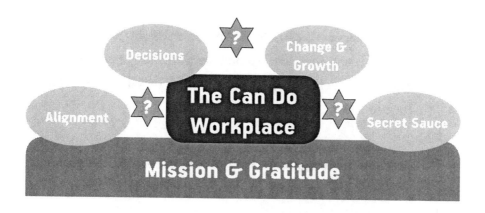

The Power & Potential of the Three "Can Do Questions"

The three "Can Do Questions" are at the center of and animate the "Can Do Model" and guide decision-making at all levels of the organization. Asking the right questions is more important than knowing the right answers. And within those right questions is where the "Can Do" energy is found and released. Asking questions is not just an important skill, it is a critical one, whether in the workplace or about your personal life.

These three questions frame decisions within a positive perspective and are always focused on the future, not looking behind. They keep the curiosity levels high and maintain a pro-active energy across the organization. The "Can Do Questions" won't let us get stuck in the muck of second-guessing or the nasty trap of guessing what we "woulda/coulda/shoulda" done differently. The three "Can Do Questions" invite engagement from all areas or departments of the organization and provide a great tool for teams, Boards, and for employees who lead and manage others.

The Three "CAN DO Questions"

1. **What can I do?** – this keeps the focus on the positive and what can happen, and off the negative and what is, or could be, going wrong.

2. **If not that, then what else can I do?** – it keeps the positive juices flowing, and sets up for Plans B, C and Z, whether they are needed or not.

3. **And, just because I can, do I?** – not everything possible is practical, healthy, or a good idea; sometimes the timing is not quite right or there needs to be one more piece in place (or taken out) before it is time to move a project forward.

The questions are designed to keep people focused on the goal, and increase curiosity and creativity in decision-making at all levels of the system. They can be used to make BIG decisions, such as researching or launching a new product line, or more routine decisions, like how to restructure schedules to reduce overtime. When used consistently, they promote routine brainstorming, not just when it's crunch time. The questions provide a dynamic difference for a traditional SWOT analysis or to help Boards think through policy decisions.

Measure twice, cut once. The last question is the gut check, created to re-measure and take one more look at a decision before moving it forward. It's the place where small, but critical changes can be made, ones that prevent misunderstandings and transform good ideas into excellent ideas. During crises when emotions are running high, it also gives individuals or a team the chance to rethink strategies and plans one more time before taking action.

Moving Organizations Toward Can Do

"Make Do" - the Enemy of Can Do: "The Can Do Workplace" model of organizational growth, is not an easy model to adopt and follow. Not at all. The elements and activities that comprise the foundation and core practices are not complicated, but neither are they easy. There are so many challenges, distractions, and detours that present themselves in the workplace, especially in the nonprofit sector, that it is quite easy to get off track. So, before we get too far down the road, let's look at some of the challenges to building a strong and sustainable "Can Do Workplace" model.

I believe that there are three primary reasons that there are not more "Can Do Workplaces":

1. People accept "OK" as a good goal, instead of pushing for the quality of "Can Do".

2. The busyness and distraction of the workaday world, what Stephen

Covey calls the "whirlwind" keeps everyone too focused on the urgency of the now so they are not focusing enough on the future.

3. The fears take hold: fear of change, fear of trusting others, fear of failure, fear of the unknown, and fear of losing face. When one or more of these fears gets added and blended into the secret sauce, it alters its taste and lowers its quality.

The net/net outcome of those situations is that the organization cannot change & grow beyond a certain point, because the change can only happen as fast as the slowest person, resulting in "Make Do", a mediocre status quo. The primary problem with "make do" is that in today's competitive, change-driven marketplace, status quo by definition means that you are moving backward on a daily basis. That is why "Make Do" anything has no place in a "Can Do Workplace".

▌ Ideas & Strategies That Help Transform Make Do into Can Do:

Be entrepreneurial: "Can Do Workplaces" operate with an entrepreneurial spirit that is goal, growth, and future-oriented. Because they value excellence and high quality in their products and services, "Can Do" leaders maintain a flexible and nimble stance with regard to growth, innovation, and change. They bring people and ideas from other industries to help plan for and develop new products and services. Those with an entrepreneurial spirit have what Carol Dweck calls a growth mindset. They read the latest articles and attend conferences, not to adopt every new idea, but to allow those ideas and the approaches to inform their thinking.

Keep Score: "Can Do Workplaces" employ effective scoreboards to track progress to goals, and have regular and transparent reporting of key indicators of success, growth, and excellence. The late Dr. Stephen Covey said it so well, "People play differently when they're keeping score." Information about "the current score" is shared across the organization in reports and meetings, and on "scorecards" displayed online and in break rooms, conference rooms, and corridors.

Honor the Ampersand: "The Can Do Model" is built around the power of the AND in the "**&**" because it helps individuals and organizations combine elements, which on some levels appear to be contradictory, messy, or disconnected, in order to achieve a positive outcome that is way above & beyond the norm. Examples include:

1. Difficult & Good – It is a myth that good = easy and great = easier! In reality, great=lots of very hard work over a long period of time. Often it feels anything but great! And, there is no endpoint or place of arrival when it switches over and becomes easy. It just becomes worth it."Can Do Workplaces" and the people who work there understand and embrace challenges as part of work required to complete the plan.

2. Change & Growth – The juncture of change & growth is at the heart of the "Can Do Workplace" because it is where the possibilities, power, and promise of greatness and excellence reside and come to life. I elaborate on this again because it is so core and so critical to the "Can Do Workplace". When change is not directly connected to growth, it creates fear and anxiety for many, and keeps organizations, teams, and individuals stuck in patterns that ensure that poor outcomes are perpetuated. On the other side of the coin, change for the sake of change is foolish. Growth in "Can Do" terms does not mean more or bigger, it only means better, healthier, and stronger.

When change is embraced and understood, people feel invited and empowered to join in and participate in shaping the growth, with a better understanding of how they benefit from the change &

growth. They learn to view, measure, and respond to internal and external fluctuations as opportunities for growth, and use lessons learned to make adjustments and course-corrections to prevent unnecessary problems. They are able to stay anchored in the possibilities, power, and promise of YES! The "&" shifts to focus to healthy options, realistic possibilities, and helps get rid of the negatives, and to take the "but" out of "Yes, but…"

3. Hear & Support Employees – "Can Do Workplaces" provide opportunities for individuals to meaningfully serve and work together in ways that meet the organization's goals, and they are provided the resources to make it happen. "Can Do Workplace" leaders believe that many people, not just a select few, have important contributions to make to the organization, and provide regular opportunities for individuals to be heard, supported, and recognized; and, thanked. Heard and listened to are the operative words. "Can Do" leaders support the employees, and don't assume that they know what is best for them or that just left to their own devices that the employees can figure things out on their own. But, they don't micromanage either. It all starts with connected relationships. When people know their roles and how they connect with others', they work harder to achieve goals that drive impact and excellence.

4. The Past & The Future– "Can Do" leaders do not blame or stay stuck in the past – or in the present – and do not waste their time on what cannot be done or "the way we used to do it here". Their focus is on moving toward the future, informed by the past. Lessons learned are revisited and shared widely as learning tools. "Can Do" leaders know that the vast majority of mistakes are not fatal, and that culling out the lessons learned provide great opportunities for individuals and groups to learn and improve performance, and not repeat the mistakes!

There are No Free Passes to "Can Do". Nowhere is this more evident than in fund development. Because of the amount of grant writing that I have done, I often meet people who imbue me with some kind of magical power. I write grant proposals, so I will find them millions of dollars from these imaginary foundations that have been waiting years just to fund them. That's Disney, not reality. All nonprofit funding is based on the combination of program or service excellence, plus relationships that have a mutual alignment with the mission. Remember, it all depends on connected relationships. I don't have the statistics, and this number varies from foundation to foundation, but it is safe to say that there are dozens of applications for every grant awarded. It is part of why I believe that the "Can Do Workplace" and its commitment to mission and excellence are so vital – to lift your organization above, or at least into strong competition with the rest. That includes commitment to maintaining a strong and vibrant infrastructure. And, if the leadership, including the Board, has not done the work of being ambassadors of the mission, and connecting the organization with the individuals, foundations or corporations, the chances of getting consistent, sustainable funding are very small indeed.

One last reminder: Never Give Up! "Can Do Workplaces" are not easy to plan, design, develop, implement, achieve, and sustain. No matter how big the budget, powerful the mission or sophisticated the strategic plan, "Can Do Workplaces" take time, unwavering commitment, discipline and infinite patience. Ironically, it is often the lessons learned on the days when it would be easier to give up that become the gems that power the next phase of change & growth.

The "Can Do Workplace" model creates a strong and dynamic foundation and framework. The "Can Do Questions" provide an ongoing cycle of inquiry that generates fresh, innovative ideas. Striving for THE BEST Secret Sauce keeps it special. But it is the intentional, daily decision to be a "Can Do Workplace" that ensures that the readiness, resources, and collaborations stay fresh, focused, and keep delivering a "Can Do" ROI. Angela Duckworth, a psychologist at the University of Pennsylvania calls this stick-to-it-tiveness, grit. She uses terms such as passion, perseverance, stamina for the work, day in and day out. Her research definition of grit is the tendency to sustain interest in and effort toward very long-term goals.[xx] Dr. Duckworth's TED Talk in April 2013[xxi] provides a great overview of this characteristic that separates successful students, West Point Cadets, salespeople and others from those not as successful. Separate Can't Do and Make Do from "Can Do".

"Can Do" is a marathon, not a sprint. The real secret to how people in organizations are able to achieve and sustain "Can Do" is found in Winston Churchill's famous quote. They "never, never, never give up!"

CHAPTER 3

MEET SOME CAN DO PEOPLE:
THE "CASE STORIES"

I believe in the power of stories to bring people, ideas, concepts, and data to life. My belief about stories also applies and about organizations, which are, after all, human collectives. So rather than presenting structured case studies at the end of the book, I am introducing you, via "case stories," to the people, mission, work, and secret sauce of four amazing nonprofits. These four organizations, each very different in their missions and work, are united in their use of the "Can Do Model", even though that was not what they called it before they met me.

My goal for including them is to inspire and motivate nonprofit leaders and managers to move out of accepting survival and average, "Can't Do" and "Make Do", as good enough and begin to believe these "Can Do" level outcomes are achievable and sustainable in your workplace.

I selected four organizations that are very diverse in their missions, geography, and organizational structure. This mix includes an organization that is seven years old and one that is almost 100 years old. Three have undergone significant organizational transformation in last five years and the change processes are included in their stories. All are service oriented; all are learning organizations; and all are currently on solid growth paths. While each is positioned to showcase a specific "Can Do" core practice, they all also embody all of four of them, and are built solidly on a foundation of mission and gratitude.

The four featured "Can Do Workplaces" are:

1. The Momentous Institute, Dallas, TX
2. Warm Heart Worldwide, Phroa, a rural village in Northern Thailand
3. The Environmental Leadership Program, Washington, DC
4. The National Head Start Association, Alexandria, VA

I present the journey of each organization through its people, and use their words to unpack their stories to let you get to know them, their work, their victories, and some of their challenges. In each, volunteers, staff, affiliates, and Board members offer unique perspectives and observations about the impact that these organizations make and the ways that the "Can Do" principles and concepts add to their impact and value.

momentous institute

Fully Aligned & Fully Alive

Delivering Exponential Impact:
Momentous Institute, Dallas, TX
(www.momentousinstitute.org)

When asked to sum up the work and mission of Momentous Institute, Executive Director Michelle Kinder says, "Momentous Institute has a singular focus: social emotional health for kids and families so they can achieve their full potential." They help the kids and families that they serve in their school and therapy centers, and then seek exponential impact, "helping kids they will never meet", by making a commitment to research, using their programs as labs and sharing their findings through partnerships and training programs across the country. At Momentous Institute, they expect - and achieve - momentous outcomes by believing they can help, and by providing tools that help all of the children they serve realize their potential for lifelong success.

The Momentous staff work with families that have some of the most painful histories and most complex needs in Dallas, and they serve these kids and their families with a dedication and spirit that focuses on possibilities and changing the odds for kids in the Dallas community and beyond. It is not just what they do, but how they do it with an intentional focus on mission, gratitude and dedication to excellence, that sets the Momentous teachers, therapists, staff, volunteers, and administrators apart.

Social Emotional Health, (SEH), is the "one true thing" that they hang their hats on, believing that SEH is critical for the health and education of children and the families, and the most effective lever to support them and their growth. According to Michelle, "what science teaches us about the brain and relationships puts the intersection of Mental Health and Education at the crux of real change." Momentous Institute works from a strengths-based approach so that parents are comforted that "my kid is not broken." Michelle adds, "We tailor our approach to the specific needs of each child and their family situation and focus on building and repairing social emotional health — developing kids who become self-regulated, good communicators, problem-solvers, empathetic, grateful, gritty and optimistic."

Since 1920, Momentous Institute has been powered by the Salesmanship Club of Dallas, a service organization of more than 600 business and community leaders who are singularly committed to transforming kids' lives. The alignment of mission to vision to values to outcomes is complete and absolute. It all starts and is sustained by connected relationships that cascade through the organization and have lasted for almost a century. This seamless alliance involves the Salesmanship Club, the Board, organizational leadership, program staff, parents, children and the wider community.

▌ Momentous Institute's

» **Mission:** Helping transform children's futures…creating new possibilities for success

» **Vision:** Social emotional health for all children, so they can achieve their full potential

» **Core Values:** Respectfulness, Stewardship, Innovation, Collaboration, Hope

Hope, hospitality, and collaboration are infused into all areas of work - with kids, families, and staff. It is noteworthy that in conversations with staff from every department, they often and easily refer to the Momentous mission, vision, and values, and use words like relentless, commitment, and intentional to describe their approach to meeting their mission.

At Momentous Institute, every member of the staff, Board, and Salesmanship Club wholly believes that:

» Children with strong social emotional health have the tools to overcome adversity.

» Families working together can break the cycles of poverty and/or abuse.

» Innovating at the intersection of mental health and education is fertile ground.

Momentous Institute, known for many years as the Salesmanship Club Youth and Family Centers, has been building and repairing social emotional health in North Texas for over 90 years. The organization serves 6,000 kids and family members directly, each year, through mental health programs and at its nationally acclaimed Momentous School. In addition to direct work with kids and families, Momentous Institute invests in

Social Emotional Health:

Within the context of one's family, community and cultural background, social and emotional health is the child's developing capacity to:

> » Form secure relationships
> » Experience and regulate emotions
> » Explore and learn

(www.zerotothree.org)

Social and emotional learning is the process through which children and adults acquire and effectively apply the knowledge, attitudes, and skills necessary to understand and manage emotions, set and achieve positive goals, feel and show empathy for others, establish and maintain positive relationships, and make responsible decisions.

SEL programming is based on the understanding that the best learning emerges in the context of supportive relationships that make learning challenging, engaging and meaningful. (Collaborative for Academic, Social, and Emotional Learning; www.casel. org)

Social emotional development is a fundamental part of a child's overall health and well-being, as it both reflects and impacts upon the developing brain's wiring and function (American Academy of Pediatrics).

research, innovative program development, and professional development and training programs - all in an effort to help many more children than they can serve directly. In 2014, they trained over 5,000 educators and clinicians, potentially impacting over 100,000 children. Research-based training is their primary growth area for the next five years in hopes of using their direct work with kids and families to inform their ability to help far more kids than they could ever serve directly.

Momentous School

"We teach children, not curriculum." At the Momentous School, (the

School), they are committed to and invest in excellence; and, it shows in exceptional and consistent ROI. By helping to build a healthy, whole child who has intrinsic motivation, they help kids and families understand the vast expansion of options available via education to make their own paths out of poverty. ***Encouraging children to meet challenging expectations communicates a belief in their potential.***

The teachers and staff understand that they have to work hard, but it is worth it because their outcomes – the children's and the School's – are excellent. They teach the children emotional self-regulation strategies alongside the academic curriculum which is written by each teacher. The School serves 248 children from age three through to grade five. Class sizes are small, limited to 12 in Pre-K and 16 per class in K-5. As many as 60% of the kids in 5th grade have been together since they were three years old. Longitudinal studies show that the Momentous School's strong, early start creates a path for success: The kids who attend the School, stay in high school and 97% graduate on time, 86% enroll in higher education, and 86% of those students persist to their sophomore year. The kids outperform their peers while at Momentous School and long after they graduate.

The Momentous School year is a long one. Teachers report to work on August 1st, and the school year runs from mid-August through the end of June. The teachers and staff develop and work hard to maintain a robust culture of academic success. Momentous School features an intensive professional development program, with weekly blocks of time dedicated to developing individualized curriculum and ongoing teacher training that addresses specific teacher goals. Momentous' School teachers and Institute staff are often trained "by the people who wrote the books," an investment that has paid for itself over and over again. This unrelenting commitment to quality by the organization helps motivate teachers to keep digging to find new and innovative ways to motivate, teach, and support the students and their families.

The hallways in the school are filled with the children's artwork and photo collages, with project boards that line the walls for as far as the eye can see. Attention to detail is evident in the small things that make a big difference: the lunch tables are smaller, circular tables with built in benches that encourage the kids to socialize during lunch, and unlike the long, rectangular tables, these smaller round tables foster inclusion instead of leaving some kids out.

Maximizing parent and family involvement in their children's education at Momentous School is not just a motto or goal, it is a commitment that is lived out daily and celebrated. Teachers make home visits before the start of each new school year and engage the entire family in the first of a series of projects that builds community and strengthens the shared caring about the children's education. The School is committed to strengthening family bonds and developing parents' confidence so they can be strong advocates for their children at home and school; and, just as important, for the parents to continue to advocate for and support their children's continued success when they leave after 5th grade to attend middle and high school in the public or charter school systems.

Each parent writes a letter to his or her "future child" that helps them clarify and articulate their goals and their dreams for their children's futures. These vision statements are also very motivating for the children. There is a parents' room in the school that is filled with dozens of family projects, where learning has taken place together. Parents are all expected to volunteer at the School during the school year and families are encouraged to network together, creating a much stronger community of families committed to their children's futures. The hope is that by seriously engaging the parents in meaningful ways, that the School's practices and approaches will scale and influence several more generations.

"Some of us call it 'school heaven,' especially when we compare Momentous' very focused environments of learning with those in the public schools," notes Sandy Nobles, Director of Education. "This level of excellence is achieved through hard work - VERY hard work - by each one of the teachers. We are very intentional about all aspects of the program, and integrate Social Emotional Health into all areas of the program in combination with our above-standards academics. Not all teachers can perform at this level, and the ones who can't choose to leave. But the teachers who are here, who stay, want to be here, and they are what makes all the difference for the children and their families."

Therapeutic Services: Transforming Lives

The Momentous Institute's therapeutic services approach is grounded in the belief that even families in great need, managing significant problems possess strengths that, when tapped, promote healing and healthier relationships. According to Fred Lines, Director of Child and Adolescent Therapy, "the work we do is about them finding a way to rediscover those strengths. Once they do, wonderful things happen!" Therapists and staff from a variety of disciplines help kids and their families develop strong relationships, improved social emotional health, and more academic success. Families work together to identify and address concerns, establish long-term solutions, and strengthen their bond and commitment. One of the best benefits of Momentous Institute's therapeutic services is that they are not limited by a managed care model with a pre-approved number of sessions. It is the Momentous model that gives the clinicians great freedom to customize the work they do with children and families in need. Therapeutic Services include individual and family therapy, treatment groups, strengths-based parent education programs, child assessments, a therapeutic afterschool program, a structured summer program, and an early childhood therapeutic program.

Momentous Institute annual family services results demonstrate the measurable impact created as lives are transformed:

» 98 percent of therapy families would recommend Momentous Institute.

» 83 percent of therapy families report their ability to manage problems has improved significantly.

One of core assumptions of their model is that almost without exception, parents want to do right by their kids. The key expectation is that people are capable of momentous outcomes and that it is our responsibility to expect momentous outcomes for all kids. The clinicians believe that they are not the experts in clients' lives and that it is critical to empower the clients to find solutions that work for them. Solutions are co-created and the family's voice is privileged over that of the therapist.

The staff understand that they must hold their judgments, opinions and ideas about the families loosely and listen to the experience of the client, respect it, and collaborate with the client to bring about the opportunity for growth. This is done by creating a safe place to give the strengths of the family a chance to emerge, so that the clients can figure their way out and become their own nexus of change, which makes their growth more powerful and meaningful for the family. According to Frankie Perez, Clinical Innovations Coordinator, "experience shows that even the heavy generational stuff gets unlocked in a way that builds skills and fosters growth."

The staffs' goal is to be "perfectly striving all the time!" The clinicians share a passion for working in strong partnership with their clients and each other, and for working hard. As part of a parallel process with families they serve, the staff recognizes its need to be in alignment to best serve the families. The Social Emotional Health model is integrated into the clinical work which is largely influenced by a post-modern approach, along with growing expertise in trauma based care, attachment theory and interpersonal neurobiology.

The clinical staff members all want to work at Momentous and serve the clients within a community mental health model. As in the school, professional development is a core function that supports excellence in clinical care. The Momentous clinicians benefit from being part of American Psychology Association-accredited pre-doctorate training program and post-doctorate psychology internship hosted by Momentous that attracts the best and brightest from around the country and is integrated directly into the staffing model. The training program incorporates a regular schedule of workshops and a speaker series throughout the year for the Momentous staff that are made available to other clinical providers across the Dallas-Fort Worth region.

Change the Odds & Expect Momentous Outcomes

The annual "*Changing the Odds Conference*" convenes the nation's top thought leaders in education and mental health, all united by a commitment to help kids achieve their full potential. The two-day conference has been wildly successful, attracting over 1,000 attendees by its third year, bringing the best and leading minds in education, parenting and behavioral health together to explore innovative solutions that help kids create a long-term success. The Momentous Institute Staff, educators, and clinicians from across the country have the chance to learn from the people who wrote the books, including Sir Ken Robinson, Malcolm Gladwell, Tina Payne Bryson, Jessica Lahey, Kevin Carroll, Daniel Pink and Paul Tough.

Honoring the Power of the Ampersand

The "Can Do" model achieves the most impact when it encourages people to accept ideas or concepts that appear to be messy contradictions or seemingly disconnected from each other, and learn how to unlock the inherent potential for growth hidden behind the contradictions. Some examples at Momentous Institute include:

» **"We work hard & that is good,"** was the sentiment echoed by staff across all departments. More than one staff shared it right up front: it's a REALLY hard place to work, and that is why I like it. "We know 'great' & 'difficult' work together to achieve more impact," was the way that Sandy Nobles stated it. "We want to ring life out of every day that we have chance to help kids." And, while it is difficult to believe, everyone on the Momentous staff wants to work there. THAT is so very rare, even for a "Can Do Workplace!"

» **Social Emotional Health & ___:** Many staff across all departments speak of the untapped potential that they see at the convergence of Social Emotional Health... & Education... & Mental Health. These powerful resources together leverage each and help staff and kids learn from the other. It is a gestalt dynamic that creates new and innovative solutions that help kids learn, grow, and heal.

» **Fail & Succeed:** Across the entire organization, strong encouragement is given to staff and kids to try new and innovative approaches to learning & growing. And, related to that, is the positive way they handle mistakes. Michelle shared, "For decades we have received a consistent message from the Salesmanship Club: 'If you can't fail, it may not be worth doing.' They strongly encourage us to push the envelope and chase innovation. When things fail they never play 'gotchya' with us, but they have extremely high expectations that we learn a lot from our failures and move forward. It's aggressive, but not sloppy." In addition to the tone set by the Salesmanship Club members, the sense of urgency is very real to Michelle and her team. They are playing the long game when it comes to Changing the Odds, but they also want things to be better for kids <u>now</u>. For the kids they see every day and for all the kids those kids represent.

Michelle says, "The price of an ambitious pace is that we might make more mistakes: we can help fewer kids and be bullet-proof – OR – we can help more kids and that may mean more mistakes. We don't want to be flippant, but we do want to be heroic in fully taking the opportunity to make a difference and sometimes that means you build the plane in mid-flight."

The staff is committed to reviewing mistakes that are made, then unpacking and using lessons learned to do better next time. At Momentous, they "fail fast and fail better," learning the lessons and moving to the next step. Michelle shared, "Problems are happening every single day – some little, some big. We can't be derailed by setbacks and we have to be very careful what meaning we ascribe to it when we do fail. Careful to check how we are thinking about ourselves, our colleagues, and the families we exist to serve. It takes an enormous commitment to look honestly at situations that don't go well, stay in the discomfort and then move through it to a better version of ourselves." They think this transparent and candid approach is not just a good model for operating the organization, but provides a great example for their clients. "We do not want to appear to be perfect; we want to be honest and show the kids and families how messy and hard it is to grow and succeed – and also how very much it is worth it."

A Momentous Transformation

Michelle says that prior to the Great Recession, the organization was very inwardly focused with core funding and great programs, so there was not much need for connections to and collaborations with the larger community. During 2008-09, they lost a significant portion of their endowment due to the economic downturn and had to cut $1M from the budget. That was a difficult and painful situation that Michelle says, "was handled wonderfully by the Board and Salesmanship Club members." The Board developed the most honorable way to address the economic downturn, then went to work studying how they would diversify revenue and how they would grow when the time came to do so. After a two-year planning process, the Club and the Board then charged Michelle and her predecessor, Delane Kinney who retired in 2012, with exploring and developing a new brand and a new model that would be "driven by opportunities" and designed to help far more kids than could ever be served directly. This charge required staff to be creative, proactive and strategic; and, one of the outcomes was the decision to re-engage with the wider community, working together to reimagine every child's potential for lifelong success. This restructuring and rebranding initiative ultimately resulted in the 2014 transformation and renaming of the organization from the Salesmanship Club Youth and Family Centers and the J. Erik Jonsson Community School to the ***Momentous Institute, Powered by the Salesmanship Club since 1920***.

After feeling the impact of the Great Recession, the Club and the Board strategically shifted and diversified their funding model. They are fortunate to have a solid and consistent revenue stream that comes from the fundraising done by the Salesmanship Club of Dallas, which includes the annual AT&T Byron Nelson PGA tournament, The Salesmanship Club Foundation, and more traditional development efforts headed up by Club members. That level of support is the reason that their clinical model can be driven by the needs of the clients, and not have managed care and insurance restrictions. That said, they do not throw money at kids or programs. In fact, their policies hold program costs to levels equal to or less than the national averages.

As part of the transformation to the new model, Momentous Institute has adopted their most aggressive strategic plan ever, where their primary areas of growth and expansion are research and training. As Michelle notes, "At the end of day, the reason why we are here is to change the odds for kids." Growth in training and research allows them to expand their reach, helping kids they will never meet. It is what they "Can Do".

Leadership

The Salesmanship Club of Dallas' core philosophy is "my success makes community more successful." Hard work to mission is modeled by the Club membership. On all levels, Momentous Institute staff understand and appreciate the fact that that they stand on the history of over 90 years of support from the Salesmanship Club. The strong relationship with the Salesmanship Club ensures that all of Momentous programs have a direct connection to the community, because Momentous Institute's Board leadership is primarily drawn from the leadership of the Salesmanship Club, who are recognized community leaders in Dallas.

The Momentous staffs' direction is shaped and influenced by concepts of servant leadership. While the organization model is as flat as it can be, boundaries are clearly marked and Michelle knows what she is responsible for, and what not to take farther; and well-defined boundaries are drawn all the way through the organization. The Board of Directors uses a policy-focused governance model, (The Carver Model). Michelle says, with a smile, that they have a healthy Board and, along with that, a great Board - CEO relationship! "They are all extraordinary and supportive, very involved without meddling! But yet, I know that they are just a phone call away if and when I need them. I'm the least stressed out Executive Director on the planet because I know who is a phone call away should we hit a bump. I know the Club has us."

Leadership opportunities are available across the organization. Frankie remarks, "In terms of conceptualizing worth or value, it really does not have to do with paycheck or title. Everyone does his or her part." Staff at all levels are provided many opportunities for project-based leadership, which provides experiential learning of leadership skills, with quick rewards and fewer risks in making a mistake.

This approach to leadership also drives how decisions are made. Critical policy decisions are made at the top; however, most decisions are made at the base, closest to the point of service. Michelle observes, "The person in the job makes decision, and we encourage that to happen, trusting peoples' judgment and experience. This approach helps keep perspective fresh and responsibility spread: it is not always the same person making all the calls." Frankie summarizes, "The Board and Salesmanship Club members have complete trust in Michelle and her team, but hold them accountable and give them full confidence and free reign to fail, which provides excellent environment to thrive."

Secret Sauce

Michelle believes that, "the secret sauce at Momentous Institute is in what gets prioritized. For us it's about prioritizing relationships, social emotional health, avoiding us/them thinking and expecting excellence at all times – from ourselves and the kids and families we exist to serve." Because it all starts with and grows stronger with connected relationships.

▌Empowered Decision Makers

Creating New Paths to Learning: Warm Heart Worldwide, Phroa, a rural village in Northern Thailand (www.warmheartworldwide.org)

Warm Heart is not a charity. "We are a community of learners that develops projects to improve access to education and basic health services, create jobs and sustainable incomes for the poorest in our villages, and restore the environment to sustain future generations. We are not experts. We honor and respect who the people are and what they know and can teach us. Our programs address acute needs by helping people learn to help themselves more effectively that before." These words are spoken dozens of times each year by Dr. D. Michael Shafer, humanitarian and retired Professor of Political Science from Rutgers University, describing the approach to work at Warm Heart Worldwide.

Warm Heart is in Chiang Mai Province, Thailand's second poorest province in the rural mountain villages, a region where young people leave in droves to work in the cities as prostitutes or laborers assembling technology products; where the people have no medicine or education; and where farmers lack clean water and have nowhere to sell their crops. "We're not about disaster relief or charity, and we don't give things away or promise outcomes," Michael says. "We will, however, embrace as many people as we can and do everything in our power so that each individual has the opportunity to do the best they can." When, with his wife Evelind Schecter, Michael founded Warm Heart in 2008, they chose the Thai phrase that means "to embrace."

Michael, always the professor, structures and describes Warm Heart as a learning organization. And, the learning involves everyone, from the villagers, to the local staff, to the dozens of volunteers each year that come to Warm Heart from around the world. Not a structured organization like IBM, or even other NGOs with experts, Warm Heart comes into these villages with notion of wanting to be part of a big experiment – to be there and present to the people and take them seriously – to ask them, "What do you really need?" "Our premise is that we are not experts and the projects are not clearly defined. Warm Heart is a group of people constantly learning about needs of people and the environment they live in, and we make the product what the needs of the people and their environment dictate. While we have great impact, we have little formalized data to report as outcomes and few evaluation metrics."

Warm Heart exists to help rural Thai villages to pull themselves out of poverty. While the approach can sound a bit free form, it is the team and the balance between Michael, college professor and dreamer, and Evelind, the operations person that makes it all work. Michael and Evelind: he, retiring after years of teaching college and organizing experiential programming around the world; and Evelind, leaving her position as Director of Specialized Business Support Services at Merck and Company, Inc., together moved to remote Thailand and founded Warm Heart. He is its President and she is the Director of Finance and Operations.

Warm Heart's mission is to tap that energy and creativity to raise the quality of life of everyone willing help themselves. They don't hand out money, things, or "solutions." They ask people what their problems and their hopes are. "What would you do if you had what it takes?"

Warm Heart is a Thai-American collaboration, with Boards of Directors in both countries and partners with other, like-minded organizations on many projects. "Building Futures Thailand", "Moondance", "Goodwill Globetrotting and Trekking for Kids", have helped transform the Warm Heart campus, and in doing so, provided a safe, warm, and nurturing environment for the children and their families. Continuing collaborations with multiple chapters of "Engineers Without Borders" provide additional clean water for village after village.

Warm Heart staff and volunteers listen and then respond to the community's definition of its problems and its solutions to them. "We hear amazing things about the challenges confronting the people of the North," Michael offers, "but who knows more than the local people what the challenges are? These people are very able to specifically define the problems they face." It is noteworthy that when the people in the villages describe the challenges they face, they do not complain about poverty. They say, "When we go south for work, we don't have the skills to get the high paying jobs. If only we could get real skills training." They do not describe their agricultural practices as failed. They say, "We can't move or cut more forest. Our fields are exhausted. Is there another crop or way to farm?"

Thailand has a well-know, devastating problem with human trafficking of its young people, both for technology jobs, which injure and disfigure their hands, and for the sex trade and prostitution, which injure and harm their souls. Dr. Shafer estimates that 80-90% is labor trafficking, rather than sex trade. Many young people see these as better options than staying at home, and worth the risks, even with the damage to their hands with jobs in technology and the shame and personal costs of participating in the sex trade. At Warm Heart, they want to offer something attractive and effective to serve as a counter point to those two industries.

Michael and Evelind intentionally opened Warm Heart in a region of Thailand where the wage rates are not high so that they could teach skills and create circumstances that would make prostitution and tech work no longer the young people's only or best option. They focus on teaching skill sets and decision-making models that address the real conditions of real people, not the cookie cutter, one-size-fits-all approach that some school and government projects use. Michael says that they work to "solve generic problems at level of motivation, not just behavior. There are lots of different answers, not just one specific one. We try to replicate the process, not the technique, designing programs that address root problems in their contexts," with what Michael calls "genericized solutions."

Four Program Areas Find and Deliver Resources the Communities Need: Warm Heart volunteers and staff collaborate with local communities to organize projects that provide equal access to quality education, basic health services, jobs, and sustainable incomes. The growth process has been iterative, both with the organization and with the people it serves, having grown in the last six years to become an integral part of the community it serves. With this hands-on approach, the programs provide capable villagers with the means to produce economically and environmentally sustainable improvements to their living standards.

Warm Heart Children's Home – The statistics are dismal: A third of Phrao children grow up on less than $1.50 a day; 15% live in mountain villages without schools, clinics or all-season roads. The social fabric of the village communities is shredded by alcohol, child abuse, disease and abandonment, and children grow up fending for themselves. Micronutrient poor diets result in birth defects almost never seen in the 21st century, and many children are so malnourished that they test below zero percentile on WHO weight-and-height-for-age growth charts. At the Warm Heart Children's Home, the children are immersed in an environment where they can thrive.

The Warm Heart philosophy and approach are simple and life changing: All children are a fresh start. Every child born into these circumstances has within himself or herself the possibility of greatness. All they need is a chance – stability, food, basic health, love, role models, and hope. In Warm Hearts words: "if only they had the opportunity to live in a nurturing environment..." In "Can Do" words: "Imagine What They Can Do!"

Education - Michael sees the long term gain, or the "spread factor" and hope inherent in educating this generation of children, rather than leaving them stuck in the hills. If he can educate 25 kids who make it through high school, five of whom go on to a university and have good health care, it creates significant positive changes for the next generation. Michael explains it this way, "So, then if each of those kids have four kids, so you are now talking about 100 people within one generation. And, then those 100 people each have four kids, we see these phenomenal changes in the life trajectory of 400 kids, a 1600% growth rate in education and income in 2 generations. This system change is what will have an impact on the Thai GDP."

One of the biggest challenges to education is that children from the tribes do not learn to speak Thai as young children. This puts them at a distinct disadvantage when they get to school. Warm Heart partners with the Khum Loi and Starfish Foundations to acquire teaching materials, and with "Always Reading Caravan" to build pre-schools in mountain villages. Even though Warm Heart is small, it possesses critical resources: partners and talented volunteers who work with the little ones and teach them Thai and English. Programs they have developed and offer as Summer Camps to local children are fun and effective for teaching English, math, and science. The volunteers also provide English language programs for adults in local government agencies, such as the police and hospital to increase their skill and professional response levels.

Public Health Projects: The challenges and barriers within the public health system in Thailand are overwhelming in communities where the elderly and people with disabilities are more or less forgotten and medical records are few and far between. Warm Heart approaches it with two models:

» At the micro level, by providing small things like eyeglasses and wheelchairs, health records for all the children, vitamins for pregnant moms, and massage therapy for seniors. And, make no mistake, those little things make HUGE differences.

» And they also approach issues at the macro level by looking at the systemic needs of the communities, especially for people with disabilities and the elderly, and testing incremental approaches with iterative steps combining the pieces over and over until they land upon effective service delivery models. Once an effective system is in place, they work to tie those improvements in health care and education back into policy in the local and regional systems.

Micro-enterprise and More– Villagers are engaged in a growing array of micro-enterprise projects, including:

» The manufacture and international distribution and sales of silk scarves, fashion accessories made from recycled resources and handmade jewelry.

» Biochar Project that teaches farmers how to produce a cheap, effective, permanent organic soil amendment that also sequesters carbon. Biochar is biomass, (rice husk, corncob), heated without oxygen, and when mixed with compost, it acts as a fertilizer that improves soil's water retention capacity, increases its ability to host beneficial microbes and fungi, improves plants' nutrient uptake, and increases yields. Warm Heart developed a low-cost, low-labor system for producing biochar from agricultural wastes, with custom "recipes" for biochar fertilizers designed for the local soils and crops.

» Farming: coffee grows happily in our mountains' poor soils and can be grown intensively. Warm Heart provides high quality, disease-resistant seedlings, helps village farmers establish nurseries, offers extension services, and guarantees market access. To ensure sustainability, Warm Heart encourages forest fruit tree cultivation, improved, small-scale corn, and legume production, in addition to the coffee.

All of the microenterprise production and skills development is accompanied by training on business fundamentals and financial literacy. "Microenterprise without business acumen does not work!" explains Michael. "Villagers need to learn the skills to get their wage rates high enough that prostitution and tech work are no longer options for them to consider."

Why Asking "Why" 100 Times and Listening Matters: Michael constantly reminds the volunteers and staff to "let the people teach you. You need to ask 'why' a hundred times and a hundred ways to fully understand the context." In working with the local people, and with the volunteers and interns, the Warm Heart approach is one that lets go of assumptions and allows people to learn to fail and then move forward with lessons learned. One example Michael offers is that the Warm Heart staff and Engineers Without Borders worked for months on a project that re-engineered cook stoves to reduce the amount of carbon monoxide and particles in the smoke that the stoves gave off in the homes and that were being inhaled in order to reduce respiratory distress and lung disease. The project was very successful. The problem is that the smoke emitted by the stoves gets rid of mosquitos that carry dengue and malaria. So rather than crafting a solution, the project resulted a disease trade off. Another example of a good idea gone wrong was a few years ago when they developed the new system to use when rotating from the rice to soy crop that was not as harmful to the soil. Rather than burn the rice stubble, they taught the farmers how to plow the field and turn the soil. The unintended consequence was that they learned that burning the rice stubble kills the insects that attack the soy; the insects came back and harmed the soy crop.

Warm Heart's Impact: Even though the approach lacks structure and the outcomes are hard to quantify, there is no doubt that since it launched on July 4th, 2008, Warm Heart, serving over 10,000 people each year in 23 programs, has had a tangible impact on breaking the cycle of poverty Chiang Mai Province.

» Warm Heart Children's Homes permit more than 37 Hill Tribe children to grow up in a warm and nurturing environment and to attend school.

» The Hill Tribe Head Start program prepares three to five year olds in remote Akha villages to attend Thai schools.

» Warm Heart Microenterprise Projects pay high dividends to local artisans.

» Water projects provide clean water daily to more than 4,500 people.

» Warm Heart distributes daily vitamins to 1,450 pregnant and nursing women and their children.

» Warm Heart Community Center in HoiSai provides the only Day Program for the Elderly and Disabled in the district of Phrao.

» Warm Heart's integrated community development project is teaching Hill Tribe villages to grow coffee while restoring watershed and reforesting mountains.

A Different Kind of Volunteer and Intern Experience:

At the heart of Warm Heart is the ever changing and often returning group of volunteers and interns who have experienced a very different kind of International Development placement. Warm Heart volunteers and interns work more than 120 volunteer months per year, providing critical support in four main project teams around the organization's programs: Operations, Education, Public Health, and Microenterprise. Team members are held accountable to one another, as well as to management. Michael says, "This means that, while we may recruit volunteers for specific positions, we expect individuals to shape these positions based on their own experiences, expertise, and resources. And, then to work together with the local people and other volunteers to make their projects and programs happen."

As Evelind, who heads up the volunteer recruitment efforts sums it up, "We serve real people with real needs and we need only volunteers ready to accept the intellectually, professionally, and personally challenging work we offer. Being a 'volunteer' at Warm Heart means only that you are not being paid for your work; it does not mean that you carry any less responsibility for the promises we have made to the people we serve. We have made commitments to our community - and we keep our commitments."

Because of the academic approach to and requirements for college intern placements, many students arrive at Warm Heart with a well-developed thesis regarding the "changes they want to help make in the world." They come with high, ingrained expectations not to fail, and a plan that contains the full set of pre-conceived notions of what has to happen while they are there. At Warm Heart, the most successful interns learn quickly that it all starts with connected relationships, and how to work "from the people up," by leveraging the lessons and experiences of these simple, but gifted local people.

Anne Bannister was a young college student from Southwestern University in Texas when she spent six months at Warm Heart, three for her college internship in Art and three months as a volunteer during the summer of 2012, just before the internship. The focus of her time was on using her photography skills to build the Warm Heart website to improve its marketing and fundraising functions. To get the quality of pictures she wanted, she spent a great deal of time with the children, building relationships that shine through her photos. "I learned a lot! Every day was a new learning experience. As much or more than learning about how to do my work at Warm Heart, I learned about myself. I worked hard because Michael pushed me to do it." When she returned to college, she staged a multimedia exhibit of her photography work, creating vignettes with bowls filled with local Thai food and village sounds. Her internship changed the direction of her life. After college, she accepted a job working in a nonprofit in the marketing department, putting to good use the skills that she learned during her time at Warm Heart.

As noted earlier, Michael sees Warm Heart as a learning organization, and so "we hire people on potential not expertise." This learning is multi-directional, coming and going and shared among the interns, the villagers and farmers in the micro-enterprise programs and the Warm Heart offices, and with the volunteers from around the world. The talents of all of these people together shape the organization and the programs it pursues. Working with Warm Heart offers lots of responsibility and opportunity, along with lots of support. Volunteers and interns who start their placement learn quickly that Warm Heart works best for individuals who have excellent interpersonal skills, and lots of initiative, patience, perseverance, and endurance.

Mistakes are tolerated, even expected as part of the large, and sometimes messy learning process. "If you tried, well, so what?" Michael asks. Volunteers, local staff, and interns alike are given the opportunities to make many decisions while working on projects, and they learn quickly that it is okay to fail. "It is scary and liberating, too," remarks Tim Dunlea, a teacher from Melbourne, Australia who, with his wife Dana, volunteered for over 10 months beginning just after they were married. "Everyone knows going in that some, even lots of projects don't work there, but continuing to try moves people closer to what will work."

When they were applying to become Warm Heart volunteers, Tim and Dana established a strong connection with Evelind. Her warmth and personal commitment to the organization, along with the fact that it is a program that did not require a fee beyond the travel to get there, were the big factors in their decision to spend the first months of their marriage in Phroa. Once they got there and saw the children's home and the living conditions, they shared their first, simultaneous reaction of, "what have we done?" immediately followed with, "this is going to be awesome!" When I asked Tim and Dana to summarize what they had learned, Tim replied in a rush of words, "We learned about ourselves, our capabilities, about mortar and concrete and paint and varnish, how to barter and negotiate and to communicate without shared language. We learned that it was sink or swim, so to always keep our heads above water." Over the Skype connection, Dana laughed her agreement.

The common thread among the volunteers and interns is their respect and admiration for Michael and Evelind, and for their commitment to the people served by Warm Heart. "Michael is a dreamer and a do-er," remarks Greg Ruccio. "His energy level carries the structure. He makes something out of nothing. Evelind balances him by ensuring that the trains run on time – that volunteers are recruited and the bills get paid. Their unique blend of talents and approach makes it all come together and work remarkably well."

Greg, with his wife Eileen and their 10 year old daughter JoJi, volunteered at Warm Heart from January to March 2013 through his company-sponsored volunteer program. When they found Warm Heart, and began to correspond with Evelind, they wanted to go there so badly that they put their all into the competition to make sure they won. Greg says that he went over to Thailand expecting to have his skills as an accountant be put to good use and wound up helping to make furniture. He believes that the amount of personal investment made by everyone on the team does very good things for the kids. And he adds, "Michael inspires people to make a difference. He and Evelind treat everyone as if they "Can Do" what is needed. They open a door to help people build their dreams, whether it's the people of Phroa or people who volunteer and intern there. It is their openness that allows this to happen."

When Tim and Dana returned to Warm Heart for a visit in early 2015, they were amazed at the progress that had been made: six more buildings had been built, there were many more kids in school and children's home. They were happy to see that the number of volunteers had increased and that there was additional infrastructure for the volunteers' projects, including a database that helps create a stronger match of skill sets and regular planning meetings. They were both very touched and delighted that people remembered them almost three years later, so they felt reassured that they had made a difference and had an impact.

Dana summarized her perspective on the core element of Warm Heart by saying Warm Heart communicates to its volunteers, "you have more value than you think you have," and that volunteers give that same message, "you have more value than you think you have," to the local people, over and over and over again.

It Takes a Village – A Slightly Different Perspective. While Michael talks often and easily about his "Can Do" approach to running Warm Heart, he and I veered off that topic to talk about what we both described as another element of "Can Do".

Michael says his friends are forever saying to him, "I wish I could do what you do." We all know that not everyone is willing to commit to the work and investment Michael and Evelind have made to Warm Heart. And, while we need to explore cloning Michael to be the new model of leader in international development, Michael and I explored several ways to encourage his friends, and all of our friends who make that statement to refocus and not let themselves off the hook quite so easily by "not knowing how."

Rather, says Michael, he believes that they need to look at their gifts and skills to discover what they "Can Do". For some it is to write a check, (as large as possible, adds Michael!). For others it is to write a blog or column to build awareness about unmet needs around the world; while for others it is to volunteer at their local soup kitchen. And, for a few, perhaps to commit six months or a year to volunteer at Warm Heart. Then, says Michael to me with a smile in his eyes, "Like Nike says, they need to Just Do It!"

Using Change to Achieve Growth

From Crisis to Scaling:

The Environmental Leadership Program (http://elpnet.org)

Small, but mighty, the Environmental Leadership Program (ELP) has harnessed the power of change & growth like few other organizations to become an exceptionally strong leader among leaders. Before getting into their story of impressive transformation, I want to set the stage and provide context by starting out with their mission, vision and work statements.

Mission: The mission of the Environmental Leadership Program is to support visionary, action-oriented, and diverse leadership for a just and sustainable future. ELP aims to catalyze change by providing emerging leaders in the diverse environmental fields with the support and guidance they need to launch new endeavors, achieve new successes, and rise to new leadership positions.

ELP's Vision of Environmental Leadership: ELP's organizational plan of action is guided by convictions about the nature of leadership and the essential role of strengths-based leadership within the environmental community:

» Leadership begins with relationships and the personal skills needed to develop them. Our greatest impact will lie in the collective capacity of the network we are creating.

» Diversity is a crucial component of public leadership. Environmental leaders must themselves reflect the diversity of the country and have the skills to work across differences.

» Leadership relies on individuals daring to take calculated professional risks.

ELP's Work: ELP is committed to building a diverse community of emerging leaders in the environmental fields and creating programs to support their development. ELP embodies its mission by:

» Offering national and regional fellowship programs that increase leadership capacity- including retreat programs for new classes of Fellows and organization-wide retreats.

» Connecting Fellows with peers through regional and national networks.

» Linking Fellows with experienced environmental leaders through substantive interactions and mentoring opportunities.

» Focusing attention on the need for the environmental community to develop the next generation of leaders.

A History of Change & Growth: The Environmental Leadership Program was founded in 1999 to prepare a new generation of leaders to work in the emerging context of interdisciplinary environmentalism. Since launching its first cohort of participants, called Fellows, in 2000, ELP has trained over 700 environmental and social change leaders from across the United States.

ELP's first major transition happened in 2005, when a planned restructuring took place consolidating its offices in New England and moving the organization to Washington, D.C. The organization's second major transition occurred in July 2008, when the founding Executive Director left for a tenured position at Yale University. During the founder's tenure, ELP had grown to be an organization of 10 employees and to a budget of almost $1 Million. ELP's third major transition took place in 2009 as a result of "The Great Recession." As the economic picture worsened and funding streams began to evaporate in the non-profit sector, ELP found itself over-staffed and underfunded - the results of which were catastrophic for the organization. By September of 2009, after layoffs and staff departures, Errol Mazursky was offered the unusual opportunity to assume the role of sole employee - as ELP's new Executive Director. On October 16, 2009, with $583 in the bank and $60,000 in debt, the rebirth of ELP as a "Can Do Organization" began.

Errol was initially hired in February 2006 as ELP's National Program Manager and had been promoted to Deputy Director in July of 2008. Having worked with a few hundred Fellows by that point, he had developed strong relationships within the community. Further, as a result of participating in ELP retreats, Errol had witnessed what he described as "life-changing learning" being experienced by people in a range of sectors - public, private, academic, and nonprofit as a result of ELP. It was through this lens of "what's possible" that Errol began the daunting task of rebuilding the organization.

In 2009, with a staff of ten, ELP was running four Regional Fellowship Programs with a total of 73 participants. Recognizing there would be no way to run four Fellowship Programs by himself in 2010, Errol made the difficult decision of moving forward with ELP's only the two most established Regional Programs and welcomed 32 new Fellows during that year. Fast forward and contrast that to 2014 when ELP, with a staff of three, ran those same two Regional Programs, added a third and launched a new National Fellowship Program with 89 Fellows joining the community of practice. ELP is now a strong and dynamic "Can Do" organization with a growing budget and eyes on further programmatic growth. In 2015, ELP will expand the knowledge and skills of over 115 emerging environmental leaders through the implementation of five regional programs and a national fellowship class - more than in any previous year - through a transformational program uniting both professional development and personal growth.

The decision in 2009 to go forward - to move through the crisis - marked what former Board Chair Kevin Bryan calls "the moment of truth for ELP." Kevin credits Errol with bringing a new, and deeply needed organizational paradigm, along with the drive, fierce determination, and willingness to do the heavy lifting required for success. Kevin recalls, "Errol personified optimism and positivity, and his great personal energy was contagious." Looking back, Errol says that one key to ELP's success was that staff and board got creative, kept the focus on long term goals, and took deliberate steps needed to get there. "We did not want to get stuck in short-term thinking; rather, we were thinking in terms of 20 years or more, knowing that things will continue to change and evolve over time. If you can dream out that far, you can see things in different ways and make better decisions."

Staffing for Leadership: In living out his and ELP's leadership beliefs and principles, Errol intentionally surrounds himself with high-functioning individuals whom he can trust, people with skills that complement his own. Today, ELP enjoys an incredibly efficient and effective three member staff which includes Jenna Ringelheim, ELP's National Programs Manager, hired in 2012; and Michael Gagné, ELP's Regional Programs Manager, who was hired in the summer of 2014. Errol provides Jenna and Michael with opportunities and flexibility to build ELP's brand and programs and then he "stays out of their way." By inviting ELP's staff to co-create the organization, and in-turn, its future, Jenna says that Errol "turns the standard work model on its head." This leadership model, while not common in many work environments, has become a signature of ELP's culture and keeps the organization agile enough to meet its needs and cultivate new opportunities. Michael says Errol "embodies total optimism and a deep belief in ELP's strengths-based leadership approach." ELP staff share a commitment to a strengths-based leadership model and have made it a core component of their curriculum to help empower ELP Fellows and enhance their work.

Before joining ELP as National Program Manager, Jenna Ringelheim was previously involved with ELP as a fellow in 2007. In the interim, Jenna filled leadership roles in several other environmental nonprofits and worked on significant ELP volunteer projects as a Senior Fellow before joining the staff in 2012. Errol jokes that when he hired Jenna, he "found someone who could take over if he got hit by a bus," which was a huge relief to him after shouldering the organization and its transition alone for three years. Jenna has an MBA with an entrepreneurial focus and brings a strong systems framework to the team. She is the one who introduced the idea of creating a Theory of Change for ELP and has worked with Michael to move its development forward. Once completed, ELP's Theory of Change will help frame and articulate the purpose and impact of the work of the organization, the Fellows, and the staff.

Michael is the newest staff member, a former nonprofit CEO with a Quaker-based social change/social justice and environmental background. He brings a much more analytical approach to the conversations and dialogue among the team. They all recognize the potential for ELP in adding Michael as the third member of the staff and are exploring strategies and growth possibilities for the future carefully and with excitement. Jenna remarks that "when Michael came on, we saw that we needed to slow down to speed up." She referred to the opportunity to clarify and test some of the deepest assumptions of the ELP process, content, and pedagogy in ways that will serve the organization long-term.

As a leadership team, Errol, Jenna, and Michael are natural network weavers which, given ELP's mission, is exactly what they need to be. They recognize that as a team and an organization they are unusually collaborative and playful in their work roles, something they truly appreciate. Michael said that one of the things that attracted him to the organization was that the job posting included: "sense of humor required (seriously!)" The ELP team is geographically diverse and distant: Errol is based in suburban Washington, DC; Michael lives just outside of Philadelphia; Jenna is in the Pacific Northwest near Portland, OR. Though they see each other at Fellows' retreats, the majority of their work together is done remotely.

Jenna feels very empowered by Errol's leadership style and, because of their organizational model and culture, is able to create space in the organization to engage and experience genuine growth "in all its glory and messiness." All three staff members talk about their appreciation for the freedom to learn and grow from mistakes, and recognize this as something that is quite rare in workplaces.

Jenna realizes that because ELP has been successful using the strengths-based leadership model, the team is now better positioned to be selective in their projects. They are also aware of how unique it is, as a small non-profit, to be able to be selective in the opportunities that they dedicate their time and talents to. Michael describes their three person team as a highly effective and efficient one, "where each one of us can follow our personal strengths, yet collectively we stay in balance."

Jenna believes that one of ELP's core strengths is the intrinsic relationship between personal and professional growth that supports people to be their whole selves in the workplace. The retreat model ELP has created goes well beyond traditional group-building dynamics such that the strong peer relationships that exist among the Fellows can – and do – translate into strengthening the wider environmental field. Their leadership training paradigm encourages the Fellows to explore both the core motivators and core fears of emerging leaders, which allows leaders to intentionally deepen their work so as to be able to build sustainable organizations in their communities. Additionally, Fellows are encouraged to actively engage with the national ELP Fellowship community long-term in order to work together to make systemic change.

Michael describes the ELP growth model as one "that allows us to test, fail/succeed, iterate, fail or succeed better, and evolve over time." From the first he learned about ELP when his wife was a Fellow, Michael felt a deep connection to ELP's values, commitment to sustainability and its work culture. He is passionate about helping people become stronger leaders = people who then return to their work with greater strength, increased tools, and capacity. By supporting these Senior Fellow change agents long-term, new insights, and tools will ripple outward and prompt positive change in other organizations.

Adding a Theory of Change: Because their work and educational model are very process-oriented, all three ELP staff agree that articulating and honing their Theory of Change, (ToC), is a critical next step in their evolution. This presentation of the logic and assumptions underlying their work will more effectively share ELP's story with prospective Fellows and Fellows' employers as well as with funders and the environmental community as a whole. In general, ToCs help make clear and convincing links between the activities of a nonprofit and the outcomes it wants to see in the world. Though ELP is early in the ToC development process, Jenna explains, "The Theory of Change provides ELP with a tool for accountability as a capacity-building organization, allowing us to look for answers about what we know about our effectiveness in leadership development." She concludes that as a result, they can begin to more consistently name the assumptions, underlying content, and organizational model, and "have answers when asked 'where is the data – qualitative and quantitative to support it?' The ToC will help with clarity, confidence, and funding." The ToC will give ELP a sound way to track and support its work – to see where the evidence is strong, identify, and fill gaps to increase their strength, the Fellows' strengths, and ultimately the wider environmental field. In our discussion, Michael shared that he sees the Theory of Change as the element that not only supports, but ensures alignment across systems as part of the Can Do Model.

Excellent Levels of Fellows' Engagement and Involvement: Errol says that the real work of ELP is an outward facing dialogue with the Fellows. By actively engaging with the community they are building, staff get a majority of their new ideas by asking the Fellows, "What do you want to see happen?" and "How can we support you to make it happen?" With the new and smaller staffing model, more Senior Fellows have become engaged with the organization in a variety of valuable capacities. Staff and Fellows believe this engagement contributes significantly to the robust health and ongoing growth of the organization.

ELP's leadership model, which is focused on engagement, creates the co-ownership communities need in order to begin addressing complex systemic challenges. In 2014, 89 of the 685 Fellows volunteered their time, totaling over 900 hours, with tasks ranging from IT support, to developing new curricula, and participating in the selection process of new Fellowship cohorts. Over 100 Fellows donated financially to support ELP and 250 (or 40%) participated in online or in-person gatherings held throughout the year. "It works," says Errol with a smile, because "the cycles of success are contagious and make Fellows want to participate and contribute more to the organization."

Kevin Bryan and Mieko Ozeki, two Senior Fellows who are very involved with ELP, say they continue to be active members of the ELP

Community because they know they are valued and appreciated, and because they are committed, together with ELP, to lifelong learning.

Kevin believes that ELP will continue to grow and prosper as long as they do not move away from their connection with the Fellows. "The Fellows own and create the core learning moments. By building these intentional experiential learning moments in an iterative way, the Fellows create or generate the next moments. The Fellows then take ownership and push ideas and initiatives into the wider environmental community."

Mieko believes there is impressive strength in the development and implementation of ELP's processes including ELP's Personal Leadership Plans, a learning method and document designed to help Fellows better balance personal life and professional growth. "The plan only works if you work it," says Mieko, which is why she takes advantage of every opportunity she is given to participate in Fellow's volunteer and leadership activities. The experiential nature of the retreats and trainings enable and encourage Fellows learn from each other. She likes the "authenticity" of the experiences that involve "little or no pretense." Mieko also agrees that Errol's positive attitude and strengths-based approach continue to be a fundamental factor in the organization's success.

Focus on Diversity: Diversity is the cornerstone of the ELP Network and is defined broadly:

- » Fellows bring a wide range of expertise.
- » Work within the non-profit, academic, business, and government sectors.
- » More "traditional" conceptions of diversity (race/ethnicity, gender, age, etc.).

ELP's commitment to diversity positions staff and Fellows to engage in challenging and fruitful conversations about "very real, and sometimes difficult" issues. These conversations bridge perspectives, areas of expertise, and open new approaches to solving problems, and create collaborations, and move the organization – and the wider environmental field – forward. Errol refers to this dynamic as being "authentic in conversations that tear down silos time and again." Kevin concludes, "Not many other organizations are willing or able to do this, but we are."

Challenges: ELP has met, and overcome many challenges in the last six years which are folded into the narrative above. The challenges ELP now faces include those of making decisions about the "how's" of going forward and both designing and embracing growth. Jenna notes that these next few years will be a "tricky period of making decisions about how we grow, with intention." Though ELP is in a position to expand, Jenna notes they will grow with care "keeping the organization lean and agile so the focus continues to be on the Fellows." Errol, Jenna, and Michael agree they will be very deliberate about adding new staff, and not move away from their successful model of high Fellows' engagement. They are in full agreement that they will not relapse into "the old ways," or allow inertia or homeostasis to set in. ELP's staff plan to stay on a growth edge which will require determination, risk, and responsibility to ensure that their growth will be both strategic and continuous.

Errol's phrase about this period in ELP's history is the title of this section: "From Crisis to Scaling". His idea of scaling is based on what he calls the "legacy model," focused not just on immediate services and programs, but on the needs ELP will be addressing 15 to 20 years from now. Errol is excited that ELP has created an organization culture where being agile and highly iterative are focal points because it allows the organization to shed ideas that are not working and replace them with new ideas and processes. The work is certainly paying off. Not only is their national community of practice growing, but funders have also begun to take notice, doubling down on their commitment to ELP and several have even delivered unsolicited and anonymous contributions.

Since the fall of 2009, ELP's Board has supported and helped Errol successfully wade through a tremendous financial crisis. Now that financial stability has been restored, all agreed that it is time to begin shifting the Board culture to one that is more entrepreneurial and equipped to encourage and support the scaling process.

What's in the Secret Sauce? Almost everyone I spoke with in the organization said that one of the most important ingredients of ELP's secret sauce is their emphasis on diversity as a way of breaking down silos within the areas of the environmental fields, from academia, to business, to government, to nonprofits, and others with interest in the environment. They also agreed that the emphasis on relationships – with a very high level of trust among staff, a remarkable level of participation among the Fellows, and unusual opportunities for ownership and leadership for both groups – creates and encourages friendships and an unusually high level of collegiality. Collectively, these ingredients of success create opportunities for significant impact on multiple levels and lasts for many years. It all starts with and grows through connected relationships.

When I asked Errol for his closing thoughts during our last conversation, he observed that as a result of working so closely with "the best of the best," he actually sees the world differently than most - it is a world "in technicolor and full of possibilities."

The Secrets of the BEST Secret Sauce

The Untiring Voice That Will Not Be Quiet: The National Head Start Association, Alexandria, VA (www.nhsa.org)

The old adage goes: everything I needed to know I learned in Kindergarten. Well, it actually starts earlier than that. Everything we need to know can be learned in Head Start! The premise of Head Start is simple:

every child, regardless of circumstances at birth, has the ability to reach their full potential.

The story of the National Head Start Association, (NHSA), is the story of its rich and meaningful relationships with the people who directly and indirectly support the over one million children and families served each year. The "secret sauce" of NHSA is how the many pieces – the Knowledge Center with member services, exceptional trainings, and tireless advocacy; the research and NHSA's committed staff – come together and work together in partnership with the Federal Office of Head Start, federal and state policy makers, the State Head Start Associations and local Head Start programs. As NHSA's Executive Director, Yasmina Vinci puts it, "Our strength is that we value partnerships and collaboration and at our core, we are relationship-based." And, always and in all ways, the focus of those relationships is on what will make a "Can Do difference" for the Head Start kids and their families. It all starts with connected relationships.

The NHSA Mission and Vision:

The National Head Start Association's mission is to coalesce, inspire, and support the Head Start field as a leader in early childhood development and education.

NHSA fulfills this mission by the promise of all possible outcomes for:

» one powerful, united Head Start voice;

» a collegial, collaborative Head Start field, one that is a valuable and valued partner and resource to early childhood development and education;

» nonpartisan support of increased Federal commitment to Head Start and, ultimately

» Healthier, empowered children and families and stronger, more vibrant communities.

…because NHSA believes that:

» all children should reach their full potential;

» every child can succeed;

» Head Start can impact the success of "at risk" children; and, that

» Quality early education fundamentally transforms children and families.

A critical element is that the mission of NHSA is not just to coalesce and support the field, but also to INSPIRE the field to tirelessly work to create a strong and sustainable future for Head Start so that it will contribute directly to the success of generations of children who might otherwise struggle throughout their lives.

The care and quality of how NHSA connects with and supports local Head Start programs is what makes it special – what makes it both a "Can Do" organization and a "Can Do Workplace". Before digging into the work and workplace elements of NHSA, it is important to understand a little about Head Start.

About Head Start

Head Start is our national commitment to give every child, regardless of circumstances at birth, an opportunity to succeed in school and in life. In the 50 years since its inception, Head Start has improved the lives of more than 32 million children and their families. Head Start alumni - or "Head Start babies," as they often call themselves - are in all walks of the nation's life. Many have grown up to become business women and men, professors, teachers, lawyers, mayors, Members of Congress, athletes, foundation Presidents, Grammy-winning musicians, poets, and parents. Wherever they are today, they remember Head Start as the place where, at an early age, they acquired a life-long love of learning.

Head Start is also the nation's laboratory for early learning innovation because it offers a unique whole child/whole family program model coupled with a delivery system that includes local programs, national standards, monitoring, professional development, and family engagement. The Head Start Model has been the basis for many other statewide and community initiatives.

What is the Head Start Model? One of the Head Start program curricula refers to the Model as "Creating an Environment of YES!" The model is comprehensive and engages the family in ways that are transformative for the children and their parents, and ultimately for the communities they live in.

The Head Start Model takes a comprehensive approach to meeting the needs of young children with its four integrated components:

1. Education that provides a wide variety of learning experiences to help children grow intellectually, socially, and emotionally.

2. Health Services, including immunizations, dental, medical, and mental health, and nutritional services that contribute to early identification of health problems.

3. Parent Involvement in planning and implementation of activities in the Head Start programming. Parents serve on policy councils and committees that make administrative decisions; participate in classes and workshops on child development; and volunteer in the classrooms and other program areas.

4. Social Services are delivered in an outreach model to determine what specific services all members of the families need, and then meet those needs.

In the Head Start Model of Parent and Family Engagement, the focus is on the healthy education, development, and growth of both the child and the family because the research repeatedly shows that personal growth of the parents positively affects the growth and development of the child. Staff help parents set and meet personal and family goals to meet their expressed needs; and, parents are invited and encouraged to participate and share decision making in every area of the local, state and national programs.

Yasmina explains that "when Head Start was launched in 1965, at its core was the idea that families and communities were integral to supporting children's successful early learning and development. Fifty years later, Head Start continues to lead in two generational approaches, always emphasizing that parents - as their children's first teachers - are a program's most important partners."

Dr. Tammy Mann, the CEO of The Campagna Center which provides Head Start programs in Alexandria, VA, echoes Yasmina's words. "People talk about the Two Generation model as if it's new. Head Start has been doing it – and doing it well – for 50 years! Head Start is where parents find their voice, see themselves as capable, achieve their goals, and reach new milestones." Within the Head Start community, parents begin doing things for themselves that they never thought they could. By becoming directly involved with the governance of the local Head Start programs, they develop skills and are provided a path to learn even more. In some communities, parents are provided access to programs and opportunities to further their education and receive support in getting jobs. Tammy continues, "The amazing thing is what happens with and for the parents – second to none across all 50 years. In an era of magic bullets, the parent involvement is the one true thing, but it requires the investment of time and energy. Head Start takes that time and invests that energy."

As a Can Do Organization:

NHSA's demonstrated strength in leadership comes from its commitment to its mission.

NHSA commits to lead: to be the untiring voice that will not be quiet until every vulnerable child is served with the Head Start model of support for the whole child, the family and the community. NHSA commits to being the one powerful, united Head Start voice that continues to be heard by working with its partners to create a collegial, collaborative Head Start field, and remaining a valuable and valued partner and resource to early childhood development and education.

Yasmina says that she thinks the most "Can Do" aspect of NHSA is "having a good mission, then keeping our commitment to pursue that mission in everything we do. NHSA is proud to be the only nonprofit national organization dedicated to supporting the transformational work of Head Start and Early Head Start. We are always looking for the possibilities and constantly navigate the tension between being true to course and turning threats into new opportunities. Every day, we witness the heroic effort that staff, teachers, and parents undertake on behalf of a million of the nation's most vulnerable children. Every day, they perform small miracles in the face of daunting obstacles to be the driver of children's healthy development and of families' economic mobility. NHSA makes sure these miracle workers' voices and stories are heard far and wide."

One of the ways NHSA leads is by positioning itself as a learning and teaching organization to be first with information and knowledge about all aspects of the early childhood field. The NHSA Knowledge Center provides the infrastructure that generates, curates, communicates, and connects knowledge across various groups to support the future of Head Start and of Head Start children. The core work of NHSA is done through four centers that support the Head Start field in both daily practice and on-going advocacy.

Center on Advocacy: The NHSA Center on Advocacy uses grassroots action, alumni and parent-driven support, and a bipartisan strategy to organize national, state, and local activities in order to ensure a successful and sustainable future for Head Start.

Center for Effective Practice: The Center for Effective Practice engages organizations committed to Head Start children and families for the purpose of identifying and sharing knowledge, creating resources for quality and innovation, and building communities of learners to deepen the impact of Head Start programs.

Center for Policy, Data, and Research: The NHSA Center for Policy, Data, and Research curates knowledge about Head Start to support Head Start programs as leaders and to share their wisdom and experience widely; generates new analyses and reflections on program and policy priorities; and strengthens dialogue and collaboration between Head Start practitioners and researchers.

Center on the States: The NHSA Center on the States cultivates, supports, and disseminates innovations and best practices in state-based early learning systems. The Center supports the work of state Head Start communities through a network of affiliates so they can be visionary leaders, trusted partners, and tireless voices for vulnerable children and families in their states.

The knowledge centers are very dynamic in nature and provide two-way information and communication channels to maintain a steady stream of input and information both from and to the field, staff, parents, and community and national partners.

And, NHSA commits to advocate: to work diligently for policy and institutional changes that ensure all vulnerable children and families have what they need to succeed. NHSA knows that it must work persistently and in concert with many other organizations to achieve and maintain nonpartisan support of sustained Federal commitment to Head Start to build healthier, empowered children and families, and stronger, more vibrant communities. Through ongoing advocacy, NHSA is able to create and promulgate a sense of urgency about the critical need to serve more vulnerable children and families. These advocacy services are provided because of, and in response to, ongoing challenges.

The challenges in meeting NHSA's mission are numerous.

First, it is a BIG field with multiple players: NHSA is the voice for over 1 million children, 200,000 staff and 1,600 Head Start grantees in the United States at any given time. Second, within the early childhood field, there are multiple stakeholders with varied viewpoints competing for public and private funding for program development and research. Because it is primarily publically funded, the Head Start Model comes under attack for political, in addition to ideological reasons on a regular basis. Also, the landscape of early childhood development and education is rapidly expanding and constantly changing, with research about brain development, social determinants of health, social emotional health, and the impacts of trauma and toxic stress adding new learning needs and opportunities every month.

When NHSA's Executive Director, Yasmina Vinci, talks about the risks to Head Start's future, she includes the tendency for people to want to do things the way they were once successful. "Just because an approach or strategy worked well before does not mean it will work now. We need to stay open and experimental, and attuned to both opportunities and threats, and to stay fresh, focused, and open to what is going on at all levels of our organization, the Head Start providers, the political arena, and the early childhood field, which taken together is our context."

At no time was this flexibility and openness as important as during the U.S. Government Sequestration in 2013-14 when the congressional cuts that were made indiscriminately to federal funds caused 57,265 kids to lose their seats in Head Start classrooms, and the kids who remained lost 1,342,015 days of service. Head Start and Early Head Start program budgets were cut $405,000,000 nationally, and more than 18,000 Head Start and Early Head Start staff lost their jobs or suffered pay cuts. In response, NHSA ignited a national grass-roots advocacy campaign, organized special events that showed how cuts impacted local communities and held a rally on the grounds of the U.S. Capitol in Washington, D.C. These interventions were incredibly effective in bringing national attention to the dire effects of the sequestration cuts. As a result of NHSA's being able to rally its grass roots base:

» 37,740 letters supporting Head Start were sent to Congress in 2013;

» 10,769 letters supporting Head Start were sent to the White House in 2013; and,

» More than 30,000 mentions of Head Start were in the media in 2013.

NHSA's advocacy leadership significantly contributed to the sequestration funds being restored, AND to getting a half-billion dollar increase in Head Start funding from Congress, plus a cost of living adjustment. The ROI was huge! Here, it is important to remember that the ROI was not for NHSA, but for the programs and suppliers who benefitted, and continue to benefit, from the restored and increased funding. Ultimately the ROI is for the most important people, the kids.

Dr. Tammy Mann offered these insights about the positive impact that NHSA achieved during Sequestration. "NHSA is willing to critically look at itself and confront the challenges in light of the political climate, which can change in an instant. Yasmina's being out there is what makes it work. Her commitment to capture the perspective of the membership, and the way that NHSA interfaces with legislators, the federal Head Start office and the Administration have had a very positive impact on the way that the program funding was restored and has been structured."

It all starts with, and is sustained by connected relationships. From start to finish and into its core, NHSA is about the kids and their families. Not about the advancement of the association or its members – it's simply, powerfully, and always about the kids, because their future success rests on the knowledge, commitment, and collaboration of families, programs, researchers, and policymakers.

As a "Can Do Workplace"

The NHSA Strategic plan truly is a core document of agency and focuses primarily on serving the field. One of its strengths, from a "Can Do" perspective, is that it recognizes the critical need for alignment all the way across the organization. Yasmina emphasizes that, "alignment takes communication. We have to look for things to bubble up, not wait for it to pop!" She focuses on staff across the organization. "We don't lead from the top not hearing what is coming from the front lines, and vice versa. Sharing information leads to better alignment."

Within NHSA, as a "Can Do Workplace", the alignment and communication are critical, as this "strategic plan is bold and aggressive and will require board, staff, field and community alignment, especially as shifts – political, economic and otherwise – threaten the families and children we serve. Creating one powerful Head Start voice means we will all have to align around the central notion that Head Start has a lasting impact, that it matters to the nation, and is worth every dollar spent."

One of the impressive things I discovered in my work with NHSA is that it puts its commitment to be a "Can Do Workplace" right into its strategic plan by stating in its organizational outcomes that as a result of the plan, **NHSA truly is a great place to work**. As a result, NHSA makes a significant investment in intentionally building and strengthening the culture of organization.

I want to share a quick personal story. I was meeting with Yasmina in her office about a project in the early fall of 2013, in the weeks just before I published the "Can Do Chronicles". She, like me, has a huge white board that occupies one of the walls of her office. The Board of Directors had approved the strategic plan a few months earlier, and she and the staff were hard at work on its implementation. What caught my eye was that in the middle of the white board, in red letters, she had written, "Be a 'Can Do' Place to Work." That started our 18-month dialogue about "Can Do" life models, attitudes, and workplaces, an ongoing conversation that has been a source of inspiration for me as I have written this book.

Another "Can Do" practice that is seen as a strength at NHSA is the realization that, as Yasmina says, "Change is constant and so we are committed to building a flexible, nimble organization that values innovation and can respond effectively to change. To embrace change, strategically is not easy," especially with such a large and diverse membership. "The first thing to do is realize majority of human kind abhors change, or will be reluctant to change." Yasmina believes that change is progress and is a good value – for her. "But ignoring the threat and dread that it presents to people in organization or constituency is very risky. As leaders, we need to understand and know when change is necessary and motivate our people to lead the change."

With so many stakeholders involved, Yasmina's biggest concern is that she does not want anyone else, except Head Start, to define Head Start. To ensure that happens, NHSA must anticipate and predict changes in program models, research outcomes, funding priorities, and more, and prepare its members to grow from the change process. The tendency is for people to want to do things the way they were once successful, what works well now and what worked well before and NHSA knows that does not work now, with technology driving change even more quickly. "We have to stay open and experimental. We cannot afford to just stay in a defensive moment of what is working in the present."

As an organization that focuses on change, NHSA leadership understands that there are more opportunities for things to go wrong and for people to make mistakes. Yasmina believes in handling mistakes constructively. In fact, she has a magnet on her fridge that reads: *Make all mistakes only once*, and so she adds, "As part of our 'Can Do' culture, we make every attempt to turn all of our mistakes into learning experiences."

This section started with discussion of relationships, and will end that way too. It is easy for a membership organization to focus on the "bigger picture issues" and lose track of the needs of the local needs of its members. Members are NHSA's greatest resource, and the staff knows it. The NHSA leadership model is shared and strengths-based, and it starts, and is based, on Head Start Parents' Councils locally. By engaging parents in the policy and decision making for their children's futures, Head Start teaches valuable life skills and ensure that the needs of those being served are being met. As a result, parent and staff voices are heard all the way through the system, allowing members at all levels to strengthen the entire network.

NHSA staff ensures that those voices are heard by continuously engaging in dialogues with local program providers via regular program and advocacy calls and extensive travel to Head Start programs across the country. Dr. Marvin Hogan, Executive Director of the Friends of Children Mississippi, which has run Head Start and Early Head Start programs for 49 years, appreciates Yasmina and the NHSA staffs' availability and willingness to "visit, sit, and be there with the people in our programs and community sends great signals and encourages others to get, and stay, involved."

Dr. Tammy Mann in Alexandria reiterates that the NHSA staff are "open to hear from the field what it thinks and expects of a membership organization. At the end of the day NHSA staff are effective, grow and thrive because they are willing to do the reciprocal dance with members."

NHSA is able to consistently be effective as the "untiring voice" with strong presence for its membership – in the field, at conferences, in Congress and the White House – because of its focus on its mission; a mission that is based on unwavering belief in the comprehensive Head Start model and its value for the children served, their families, and the communities they live in.

CHAPTER 4

INGREDIENTS AND TIPS TO ENHANCE YOUR SECRET SAUCE

Take a few moments and think about your favorite meal, a delicious recipe or the best entrée at your favorite restaurant. What makes them special? For me, I think of this little Italian restaurant in Worcester, MA that has just the best combination of olive oil and spices in its bread dipping sauce. This sauce is so special and tasty that I have used it numerous times as a salad dressing and over pasta, too. I never tire of it.

Writing about this also makes me think of my twin cousins Joan and Jane and their husbands who are wonderful friends as well as relatives. One thing that hubbies Jeff and Allen both do exceptionally well is BBQ. Jeff does brisket to perfection and Allen does ribs to die for. Allen has a Big Green Egg ceramic grill and Jeff has one of his own design. Both take great pride in their prep for these feasts and neither one of them takes a single short cut in the process. In fact, for these melt in your mouth creations, both spend hours blending and marinating and then basting while they cook. I have to fly to San Jose for the brisket and Dallas for the ribs, but their secret sauces are well worth the airfare!

The secret sauce of on a juicy rack of ribs is pretty easy to understand. But the secret sauce of an organization…what is that, exactly? The Secret Sauce in a "Can Do Workplace" is the signature quality of the organization that makes its culture special and sets it apart from other places to work. It is the "je ne sais quoi" that attracts good people to, and keeps them in an organization. And, it all starts with, and is made richer by far within connected relationships. The secret sauce is the product of how the people who populate the organization's systems work together and how they value and treat each other and the people whom they serve; that is what creates, blends, and brands their secret sauce. This sauce seeps inside and saturates the entire organization. The "Can Do" foundation elements, (mission and gratitude), and framework, (four practices and questions), provide strength and support to the systems, but it is the secret sauce that pulls it all together to animate and drive a "Can Do Workplace" toward reaching its goals and making a positive impact.

THE BEST secret sauce is what makes people really want to work there, and invest the time and push and/or pull extra hard to help reach excellent outcomes, over and over again. It is also what attracts and keeps clients and partners and helps them achieve their goals.

Even THE BEST secret sauce can and will change over time – for better or for worse! Some changes happen by mistake. Even, and especially during times when the alignment is smooth and the innovation is working and everyone has the resources they need. That is when the temptation is to believe "it doesn't get any better than this!" and then people start to focus on other things. And, perhaps it doesn't get any better, but if everyone doesn't keep paying intentional attention to those practices, things will start to slip, and pretty soon, the sauce has lost its THE BEST Sauce zing!

In the pages that follow, I will share ideas and some of the "cooks' secrets" on making your secret sauce awesome sauce! In addition to my own perspectives, I have included some hints from the group of Executive Directors, CEOs, and Board Members I interviewed and from some experts in the nonprofit field.

Don't Take Shortcuts or Cut Corners

One of the most important things to know about how to put and keep the quality in a great secret sauce is that the people in "Can Do Workplaces" don't take shortcuts. When the shortcuts are taken and quality is reduced, the secret sauce gets watered down and is not THE BEST or so special anymore. Creating a "Can Do Workplace" requires the best of everyone giving 100% plus. Sure people have off days, but the ones that are committed to quality don't slack off – that's different.

Stephen Covey in his book, "First Things First," talks about the Law of the Farm to illustrate the how important it is not to take shortcuts. "Can you imagine forgetting to plant in the spring, flaking out all summer and hitting it hard in the fall – and expecting to get a bountiful harvest overnight?...There's no way to fake the harvest."[xxii]

Sometimes, when it is necessary to have cuts made to budget or services, it can be tempting to cut all of the "low hanging fruit" or make across-the-board reductions. It takes more time and thought to make strategic cuts, but this careful approach allows more of THE BEST parts of the secret sauce to survive, and provides more opportunities to rebound. Don't take shortcuts!

Develop and Practice Strength-Based Servant Leadership

As I was writing this section of the book, I learned that Marva Collins passed away. Ms. Collins was the fiery, passionate, and committed Black educator who quit her job as a teacher in the Chicago Public Schools founded the Westside Preparatory School in Chicago in 1975. Her schools and her method flourished and became nationally known for success in taking children from impoverished neighborhoods who were labeled unteachable and turning them into some of the best students. Carol Dweck, in her book, *Mindset: The New Psycholo-*

gy of Success," tells the story of Marva saying to a young boy named Freddie on the first day of school, "I am not going to let you fail."[xxiii] The support, care and commitment to meeting his needs communicated within that statement are powerful. When I think of the messages that engaged leaders need to give to their employees and teams, I think of Marva – "I am not going to let you fail." When I think of the messages that strong, "Can Do" nonprofits need to give to the people they serve, I think of Marva – "I am not going to let you fail." It is a commitment to work together, to ensure that the goals are both ambitious and reality-based, and that there are adequate resources and support sufficient for everyone to succeed.

Authentic servant leaders ensure that the people served by their organizations, be they kids, families, those seeking medical or food services, other providers, advocates, educators, whomever, are as fully engaged as possible with the organization, in partnership with the leadership and the staff. This is in strong contrast to a top-down, "expert to the rescue" model that often becomes activated and then institutionalized, sometimes without people being consciously aware of it. Nonprofit leadership goes well beyond the Executive Director or CEO and includes the Board as ambassadors for the mission into the community while representing the community living out its commitment to the mission. The most important connection that the leadership and staff of a nonprofit have is with the people that they serve; and, it is critical that these leaders and staff believe in the inherent strengths, dignity, and worth of their clients and really listen them, and to strive to provide products and services that help those served to meet their needs.

"Empower people to say YES! Make sure they know and understand rules of the game and are empowered to say yes!"-Tom Pié, Board of Directors, St. John's Home, Wheeling, WV [xxiv]

An entrepreneurial spirit is another attribute of authentic servant leaders that makes a huge "Can Do" difference for the organization and the people it serves. It is an approach to doing work and to the organization's health that balances innovation and growth with risk management. In an article in INC. Magazine, Matt Ehrlichman, Founder and CEO of Porch. com, says that an entrepreneurial spirit "develops in the individuals who demonstrate a true passion for building something great from nothing and they are willing to push themselves to the limits to achieve big goals."[xxv] In his article, Ehrlichman provides five indicators of someone who possesses an entrepreneurial spirit: 1) they are in tune with their passion; 2) they always question how it can be done better; 3) they are optimist about possibilities; 4) they are willing to take calculated risks; and, 5) most of all, they execute.[xxvi]

I like that Ehrlichman emphasizes two things that are important to my working definition of entrepreneurial spirit: These leaders keep and share a sense of curiosity to learn about what else is out there and find out "how it can make what we do better," and they execute, which balances doing with thinking. I want to add that I also believe that those with an entrepreneurial spirit laugh more and have more fun doing their work, even when they are working very hard!

In his classic, "**Good to Great**," Jim Collins explores Level 5 Leadership, and clarifies that what distinguishes them from other leaders is that "they are ambitious, first and foremost, for the cause, the movement, the mission, the work – not themselves – and they have the will to do whatever it takes, (whatever it takes), to make good on that ambition. In the social sector, the Level 5's compelling combination of personal humility and professional will is a key factor in creating legitimacy and influence."[xxvii] In a nonprofit sector, it means putting needs of the people being served first, and keeping them first. The nonprofit leaders' influence is applied thoughtfully and strategically with a variety of stakeholders, including the

Board, the staff, the funders, the community, and the clients, to make the best decisions to advance the mission. The whole leadership team works from its combined strengths.

In their, *"Strengths-Based Leadership: Great Leaders, Teams and Why People Follow,"* Tom Rath and Barry Conchie begin their book with the results of extensive research on leadership using Gallup results and their own study. Their three key findings are that the most effective leaders: 1) are always investing in strengths; 2) surround themselves with the right people and then maximize their team; 3) understand their followers' needs. Or, in "Can Do" terms, authentic strength-based servant leadership starts with, and stays grounded in connected relationships.

Just to clarify, being a strong servant leader is not about being perfect. Rather, it is grounded in reality. Servant leadership is about making an enduring commitment to the mission and the people, and then making sure you learn, know, and get what you need to do your job, serving as a role model for the rest of the staff and the Board. When servant leaders make a mistake, and they all do, they own it right away, learn from it, and freely share those lessons learned to help others avoid those mistakes. And, then move on.

Authentic servant leaders keep growing. Ron Freidman, in his new book, *"The Best Place to Work: The Art and Science of Creating an Extraordinary Workplace,"* talks about the importance of the learning curve. "It's by walking the precipice between your current abilities and the skills just beyond your reach that growth happens. Master performers don't get to where they are by playing at the same level day after day. They do so by risking failure and using the feedback to master new skills…. Failure, per se, is not enough. The important thing is to mine the failure for insight that can improve your next attempt."[xxviii]

Being an effective "Can Do" leader requires a huge personal and professional investment to excellence and success, and so it also requires an equally huge commitment to health and balance. "Can Do" leaders have strategies to stay healthy, focused, and develop strong support systems so that they don't risk burning out. Few things can sour an organization's secret sauce more than a leader who has burned out. It hurts and is painful for the leader, the organization, and the people being served. I have experienced this personally and share some of my lessons learned about the importance of preventing burnout in Chapter 5.

▌ The Roles of Motivated & Skilled Managers

A great nonprofit manager is the communicator and advocate of shared ownership of the mission up, down, and across an organization. Managers, by definition, are in the middle and they can create great flow or block it all up. Management is one of the areas in an organization where great attention creates excellent outcomes and lack of attention causes dangerous disruptions.

The role of the managers, according to Allison Green and Jerry Hauser in "*Managing to Change the World: The Nonprofit Manager's Guide to Getting Results,*" is to do just that, get results. Managers are be responsible not just for products, but for people. People that get results. Managers, they argue, do this best by "being clear about what they expect, helping people meet the manager's and the organization's expectations, ensuring people are in roles in which they excel, and getting everyone aligned around a common purpose, build their staff's morale in the long run."[xxix]

Leadership guru John W. Gardner reminds us that "teachers and leaders share a trade secret – that when they expect high performance of their charges, they increase the likelihood of high performance. If you expect me to hold myself to standards of excellent and discipline, you increase the likelihood that I will do so."[xxx]

About Effective Managers: "*I try to recognize, empower, and appreciate my people. I keep no hidden agendas and let them be safe so that they can shine! If they shine, we all shine. The best thing a director can do is recognize the achievements of managers and have success attributed to them! More I can point to staff and recognize my team, the more we all look good.*"*- Frank Juliano, Executive Director, Reeves-Reed Arboretum, Summit, NJ*

Leaders in "Can Do Workplaces" provide managers with numerous and varied opportunities to be included in key organizational discussions and decisions, even if it is to participate to answer the question: "This is what we are going to do – how can we do it in a way that promotes the best outcomes and prevents problems, error and resistance?" And, managers provide similar opportunities for the employees they supervise to provide input as often as possible.

Managers play a critical role in the level of employee engagement across the organization. One of the key findings of the Gallup Report, *"State of the American Workplace: Employee Engagement Insights for U.S. Business Leaders,"* is that managers who focus on their employees' strengths can practically eliminate active disengagement and double the average of U.S. workers who are engaged nationwide.[xxxi]

A key ingredient to the managers', and the organization's, success is making sure that expectations are clearly communicated up and down, from leadership through managers to line staff, and back up through the system. And, it is very important that managers are provided the resources that they need, including training, supervision, mentoring, coaching, and support for improving their decision-making skills. There are few other investments as important because, in the long term, strong managers become a pipeline for emerging leadership.

It is critical for the health of the overall organization that managers be given the opportunity to reveal, then learn from, their mistakes and grow. If that is not possible, or they feel that it is not possible to reveal and discuss their mistakes, they will hide their errors and risk creating service and safety gaps and potential for systems failure. In human services agencies, this means real people, including kids, can get hurt.

Green and Hauser emphasize the need for, and potential in building quality managers in nonprofits. "Given what nonprofits do, we have a moral imperative to commit to strong, effective management practices because what's at stake is much more important than a business's bottom line."[xxxii]

Maintain an Infrastructure that Supports Excellence

Like having strong bones in your body or a strong foundation in your home, a strong infrastructure supports and is a catalyst for health in an organization, and a critical ingredient to achieving and sustaining excellence and success. My definition of infrastructure includes the financial, management and administrative systems, HR policies and procedures, risk management resources, and the activities around assessment of needs and measuring outcomes. All of the systems that support the quality and sustainability of the programs or services delivered. They are not the fun, sexy, or glamorous parts of the organization that are "out there" where the public can see them and how they operate. Their less than glamorous and visible nature does not excuse not paying attention to them, because like the pipes in our house, they are what keep the good moving forward and the bad moving out.

In recent years, there has been a great deal of attention in the sector, primarily from the funders about what percentage of the budget is allocated to these activities, along with a strong push to keep those percentages low. There is also an inclination for funders to want to fund programs or capital, and not being inclined or willing to fund these internal activities of the organization, a trend that is very bothersome and worrisome to me. No matter how well aligned an organization is to its mission, how great the services being provided are, if the infrastructure is not consistently maintained and enhanced, the operation of the organization can and will drift out of alignment and create significant damage and pose a real risk to its future. I have included a case study of such an organization in Chapter 5.

Use Your Data and Keep Scoreboards

Working to data-driven outcomes, both program and fiscal is still a difficult approach to implement for some nonprofits. The staff knows that it is expected, but are unclear about how to do it correctly; they struggle with competing priorities or they get so lost in what Stephen Covey calls the "whirlwind," that they forget to do the measuring until it is too late. Sometimes, they actually fail to measure what is an excellent, so there is little to show the funders for the excellent work they have done.

For "Can Do Workplaces", the data management and dissemination and the program outcome assessment processes are 24/7/365 activities. It is easy for these somewhat boring, detailed activities to get lost if they are not built into the core of the organization calendar because one or more of the following, all too predictable things can happen: staff gets busy with people and programs and forgets about the measures, or some of the pre-measures are not completed, rendering the post-program measures meaningless. Someone gets sick and a required element of a program is not delivered.

Using scoreboards helps keep everyone on the same page. The first question someone asks when they come late to a football game or other sports event, or when they return from the snack bar is: "what is the score?" One way to keep staff engaged and motivated to meet goals is to create and maintain, (that can be the tricky part!), a scoreboard for measuring progress to goals. In football they don't turn the scoreboard off in the third quarter and back on in the fourth or stop tracking first downs and yardage. The scoreboard is on for the entire game, tracking and telling everyone all of the key indicators that inform the score. It just makes sense to keep everyone informed all the way through a program year or project, eliminating surprises, which often are not good ones, at the end of the year.

Scoreboards can vary from simple spreadsheets on a share drive to white boards in break rooms with monthly-outcomes-to-goal figures and charts. The important "Can Do" aspects are that they are easily understood by everyone, that the data reflected are core data that drive the outcomes, and that the scoreboards are designed in ways that motivate, not punish.

The Critical Role of Communication

While communication has been integrated into the other areas in this chapter and throughout the book, it needs to get some special attention here. Strong communication systems, and when appropriate, a focused communication plan, are critical components of a "Can Do Workplace" that really impact the quality of the organization's secret sauce.

Effective communication systems are important in organizations all of the time, but especially so during times of transition. "Can Do Workplaces" make it a priority to keep the lines of communication open as a basic practice so that they are not trying to create a communication system during a time of change or crisis. Consistent written and verbal communication about changes and schedules and expectations helps diminish anxiety and reduce negative outcomes.

Nature abhors a vacuum, so it is important to remember that the lack of positive or productive communication within an organization, especially during a time of transition, can lead to the generation of negative communication to fill its place. Most of the time, staff is not intending to be mean or to hurt the organization. However, when fear grows and peoples' anxiety level heightens, negative, gossipy communication can move through an organization faster than the speed of light; faster, even, than an announcement about unilateral pay raises.

Environmental cues are also important parts of organizational communication. Values, mission, welcome, and comfort can be communicated visually, such as through the children's art work in the Momentous Institute and Warm Heart classrooms and hallways, or with motivational posters in conference rooms, or quotes from the strategic plan lining the hallways. These visuals help reinforce the verbal and written communications, help keep the focus on the mission and, in the example of Momentous Institute and Warm Heart, communicate a deep level of respect and caring for the children they serve. Positive organizational environments also help prevent misuse of property and small destructive acts, such as graffiti, which is important when serving at-risk populations.

Overcoming Resistance to Change

Change is not easy. One of the things that distinguishes "Can Do Workplaces" from others is that their leaders stay ahead of change and help staff be deliberate in predicting, planning for, working with and through, and growing from change. Some organizations move to the discussion level about change, and then stop. Talking about change is not making change. Change is about action and ongoing execution. To be most effectively executed, change needs to be managed, tracked, course-corrected, not once, not three times, but continuously.

On Change: "*Everyone should be very open to the need to change! Create a culture of continuous innovation to appreciate, understand embrace and lead change, not let change happen to us.*" *-Robert M. Sheehan, Jr. Lecturer & Academic Director of the Executive MBA Program, University of Maryland*

"Communicate expectations and status updates, over and over again." Seth Godin explains his support for expectations this way. "Expectations aren't guarantees, but expectations give us the chance to act as if, to trade now for later, to invest in hard work and productive dreaming on our way to making an impact. Expectations work for two reasons. First, they give us the enthusiasm and confidence to do hard work. Second, like a placebo, they subtly change our attitude, and give us the resilience to make it through the rough spots. 'Eventually' gives us the energy to persist."[xxxiii]

More on Change: Change is scary! When we are going someplace I am not prepared to go, change can be misinterpreted as doing something wrong and feel like criticism. My organization is okay with change provided that there is trust – and that the people feel safe!"- Frank Juliano, Executive Director, Reeves-Reed Arboretum, Summit, NJ [xxxiv]

For change to happen most effectively, "Can Do" leaders create and communicate the parameters, boundaries and timelines. They do this communicating personally as well as in written and recorded formats. Smart leaders ask questions and get feedback while preparing for change, to ensure that the messages being sent are received and interpreted as intended. It is also important to make any consequences for resisting or refusing change – for individuals, teams, and the organization – known ahead of time; and then to follow through with the consequences.

"Embrace change and see it as opportunity and not accept status quo. Celebrate success and figure out what next."- Errol Mazursky, Executive Director, Environmental Leadership Project, Greenbelt, MD [xxxv]

As has been suggested in other parts of the book, take a "baby steps" approach to change whenever possible. This allows the people impacted to reflect on specific aspects of change and then prepare to take the next steps in the process. Once you have moved more than 60% of the way through the entire change process, it is helpful to pause to look back at the amount of progress that has been made, keeping the focus on the positives and lessons learned to help increase motivation and prepare to make the remainder of the changes.

Something that is often overlooked is that the change process can be "paused" when needed. The reason for and duration of the pause should to be well communicated to all relevant stakeholders. Just before the last phase of the big transformation at Momentous Institute, Michelle Kinder, their Executive Director realized that the staff in the satellite center was not ready for the next big step, which was the public announcement of the name and brand change. "They felt out of the loop, and unready for what was next. It felt like an avalanche coming toward them." The very tough, but correct decision was made to postpone the big public announcement until communications and trust was rebuilt and the staff at that center felt equipped and ready to deal with the change. Remember, it is much better to have a short delay than a catastrophe.

CHAPTER 5

LESSONS LEARNED FROM "CAN'T DO" - FOUR CASE STUDIES

I woke up in the middle of the night recently asking myself, "How can I write this book when I have had so many "Can't Do" moments and made so many mistakes?" Clearly, there have been many times when, as a manager, Executive Director, CEO and consultant that I have not done the things I write about here. Not just a couple - many! Well, a huge benefit to being a leader who advocates for the power of change & growth is that I am constantly finding new ways to take some of the mistakes I have made, or that I have become aware of first hand, study them and use these lessons learned to coach and teach other nonprofit leaders and managers. Because it is often easier to learn from the stories of others, I include four case studies that address some of my most important lessons learned as they relate to each of the core "Can Do" practices.

Like so many other nonprofit professionals, I approach every day with the same two-part commitment: to do the best that I can in each situation with the resources and knowledge I have available; and, to never stop learning. Before I present and discuss these lessons learned, I want to share some context and my assumptions. These are my perceptions of events that shaped my career and are based on my experiences. At the time I was trying to do my best, and I want to, and ask you to give the other people discussed – and me! – a very generous benefit of the doubt, great latitude, and abundant grace. In telling these stories, I am trying to be fair while being transparent, and sometime it is a tricky balance. Please remember that there is much more to each story and to the people represented. Each of these case studies represents only part of a much larger and complex situation, culled out to emphasize a specific issue or aspect of the work, and experience of the lifecycle of an organization.

These case studies have been difficult to write, but very healing. My recommendation is to think back through the specifics of times you wish you could have a "do over," searching for the lessons learned and then write it up as a case study, like I have, trying to be objective and allow for others' perspectives to be represented. When discussing these case studies, a colleague of mine reflected, "Last year when I was on a leadership search committee, one of the questions that came up for applicants was this: 'What is the biggest mistake you ever made in your career, and if given the chance, how would you have handled the situation differently?' Same idea, great question!" I hope that you discover, as I have found, that the ROI of doing this exercise is remarkable.

Alignment

The following case story portrays the very unfortunate outcome for an organization when accountability breaks down and the alignment sight line becomes filled with gaps that quietly grow and then fester.

All Leaders Must Know About and Pay Attention to the Infrastructure: When I first started outlining this book, I never imagined writing this section at all. It would be like saying be sure you put the plumbing in the plans for the award-winning house! Then, I learned first-hand that ensuring full alignment requires that the entire leadership team pay attention to the organizational infrastructure consistently; not accept substitutes for key reporting requirements; and, to consistently track and adhere to compliance deadlines.

Let me introduce this section with a brief, recent personal story from my family. My dad loved his home so much that we joked that he loved it more than he loved us. It is a beautiful home located on just over half an acre on The Ohio State University's Golf Course, and he was able to live there until just three weeks before he died. Now, following my dad's death last year, our family home of 40 years belongs to a wonderful young family whom we hope will create wonderful memories enjoying its large entertainment areas, wonderful yard and the pool. The path to selling that house was not an easy one for me and my siblings. Why? Because my dad did not invest in maintaining the infrastructure after my mother's death fourteen years earlier. For example, (just one of many!), about 10 years before his death, he discovered a leak in the chimney which he remedied by installing a chimney cap. The problem is that it was a small structural crack, which after 10 years grew to become a much larger structural crack; and then the water draining down between the chimney and the walls had also rotted the floor and subfloor of the family room. The first appraiser did not see it – the floor is carpeted and the damage was hidden. The new owner's home inspector sure did see it, and between the repair of the much larger crack and fixing the floor, it cost us about $25,000 in give backs to the buyer. Rightly so, but painful nonetheless. And, totally preventable.

The same thing can happen in an organization. We love the mission and the work so much that we don't adequately attend to or invest in the infrastructure – the fiscal systems, the HR and operation policies and procedures, the amount of insurance, the review of the vendors' pricing and quality – to ensure that the organization's "guts" are healthy. With focus on our clients and the pressure of producing impact and maintaining funding, we might take shortcuts and make cutbacks to the operating systems as a way to save money. Add to that the fact that many funders will only fund programs and there is great pressure to keep indirect costs down, making it is easier to cut back in that area. Organizational leaders keep piecing things together, and it seems to be working fine. Until, one day, we can't piece it together anymore because one or more of the core systems that has been neglected fails, and the whole organization, and the people it serves, pay the price. Then, when it happens, many people are surprised and say, "The quality of the work is so great, how could this happen?" The answer is that sometimes we, (staff, clients, Board members, funding sources), don't value these aspects of the organization in the same way that we value the programs and outcome and impact data of that organization.

If you observed or participated in the programs that were delivered by a small health education nonprofit in my hometown, I know you would have been very impressed. The Executive Director and staff paid close attention to detail and delivered very high quality and innovative programming. In fact, they were asked to help scale one of the projects that they did for a government partner. National leaders publically praised their work and one of their events received coveted coverage on the local new channel. For all appearances, they were really a "Can Do" kind of organization.

Cash-flow challenges were regularly discussed at Board meetings, but they were a small staff and very busy, so it was almost taken for granted. The organization had grown enough to require an audit in addition to the IRS 990; that was discussed at Board meetings, but not followed through on between meetings. New programs and funding strategies were being developed and that was the focus of the Executive Director's attention and Board reports. That was until she got a great new job and resigned. From the start of the transition, gaps in the infrastructure began to become evident, catching everyone unawares about their size and scope. One of the things that had been put to the side was the accounting software. The Board was told it had to be upgraded and it would be done when cash flow improved. That never happened and so the organization ran without a ledger of accounts and standard financial reports for over two years. During those two years, the Executive Director used spreadsheets to present financials to the Board and, from those reports, the contracts and receivables appeared to the Board to be sufficient to support the organization. And, after all was said and done, the bottom line is that the contracts were sufficient and the agency was, after all was accounted for, financially solvent.

The cash flow issues were primarily caused by very irregular and late billing practices, one of the things that the staff were "too busy" to keep current. As a result, when I started as Interim Executive Director, there was over $75,000 in aged, but unbilled receivables against a budget of just under $600,000 a year; and another $40,000 that should have been billed before the former Executive Director left. Part of the problem was that each of the billings needed to be done in great detail, with specific expenses reconciled and allocated to each of the grants. Without monthly financial reconciliations, this was a very time consuming project that was primarily done using the monthly bank account statements. During the "shortest on cash flow" months leading up to her departure, the Executive Director had not paid the phone/internet/wireless bill, the attorney or for several of the employee benefits; and she issued a few paychecks with net amount checks drawn on the regular bank account, not through payroll. The result was that the phone had been totally shut down so no one could request services, the payroll required an expensive adjustment with a back tax bill, and it was going to cost thousands of dollars to recreate and clean up the ledger of accounts.

What sadly sealed the demise and dissolution of this organization was the IRS action that automatically revoked the organization's 501(c)(3) status, which had become effective 60 days prior to my arrival. At the end of my third week as Interim Executive Director, I called the IRS to check on the status of the 990 filings. I had a hard copy of the one from three years previous, but did not see it reflected on Guidestar's website, the go-to location to find nonprofit IRS990s. The gentleman at the IRS confirmed that it had not been filed and that the automatic revocation was already in effect. If an IRS990 is not filed for three consecutive years, it is automatically revoked four months and fifteen days later, which is what had happened. What I discovered later that day was that while the IRS 990 had been completed for the third year previous, the final step to file is with the IRS had not been taken. The work had been done, the form had been signed, but not returned to the CPAs and, therefore, not filed. This small detail that they were too busy to follow through on proved fatal. There were other areas within the infrastructure of organization, which I am not going to detail here, where there were, if I can borrow the metaphor from my father's house, rotten floorboards covered by carpet.

I delivered the sad news to the Board later that evening, a Friday; and, at their direction, I notified all of the program partners the following Monday. All of the agency's contracts required that the organization be a 501(c)(3) in good standing; and so each partner issued a stop work order that week. And, each of the program partners was, to a person, stunned by what had happened. "They went the extra mile for us." "Their ideas and implementation were phenomenal." "Their trainings were excellent, both development and delivery." While the 501(c)(3) status could have been restored, it would have cost much more than the agency could afford, given all of the back accounting work that would have to be done, plus the cost of two more IRS 990s and an audit. Additionally, since all work was stopped on existing contracts because of losing the 501(c)(3) status, there was the real risk of not being able to re-engage with those funding partners if/when it was restored. The patient was on life support when I arrived; the revocation of the 501(c)(3) status was the final, irreversible setback. We pulled the plug.

There had been numerous gaps and disconnects in the organization's alignment that grew over time. The importance and commitment to quality placed on the services was in stark contrast with and totally disconnected from the lack of value placed on the infrastructure to support those services. The reports to the Board and partners obscured the gaps in the fiscal integrity of the agency under layers of busyness and competing priorities.

There are hundreds of lessons to be learned from this very brief case study. Many people asked me pointed questions during the months it took to disassemble the agency and dissolve the corporation. Here are my answers:

1. While their intentions and energy were good and well intentioned, focused on mission and providing good programs to a very high need community, the Board and Executive Director kept putting off critical compliance activities without appreciating that these delays held huge consequences.

2. Yes, the Board could/should have forced the issue with the financials, but the reports developed by the Executive Director were very effective and convincing. The Board only met twice a year and her "rising star" status in the community made her requests to delay meetings and excuses of "not getting around to" moving things forward hard to argue with.

3. The goal, and what became my top priority was to close the agency in a way that ensured that the needs of the partners, contractors, vendors and clients were met with high quality and integrity while honoring the good work that had been done through the years. My biggest relief is that the agency was sufficiently financially solvent to allow this goal to be achieved.

When a Board hires an Executive Director, it needs to ensure that he or she has a full understanding of all of the aspects of and skills or resources to carry out the responsibilities in that role. If an Executive, as it sometimes happens, is hired for specific strengths, to ensure that there are resources, such as senior staff with complementary skills or contracted service available and put in place in the areas to fill the gaps. Both the Executive Director and Board are accountable, in slightly different, but complementary ways, for the fiscal health and integrity of the agency. My reason for sharing this story is to remind nonprofit Board and leaders about how tragic the consequences of the "rotten floorboards covered with carpet" syndrome can be. Every nonprofit Board member and the Executive Director or CEO are responsible for being knowledgeable of all federal, state, and local compliance requirements, and consequences, related to their corporations, and to understand the scope of their fiduciary responsibilities. This is just as important, if not more so than seeking and obtaining new funding and contracts, because it lays the foundation upon which those contracts and programs will operate, kind of like the floorboards support the furnishings and people living in a home.

Decision-Making

One of critical requirements of strength-based leaders is that they are able to trust their staff to make decisions related to their work product. This includes understanding that staff make mistakes at times, and providing them opportunities to recover, learn, and grow from these experiences. The polar opposite, which is fear-based leadership, creates systemic problems that erode employee confidence and jeopardize the effectiveness of the organization's work product. Fear-based leadership becomes evident when an Executive Director or other key leader is in over his or her head, has serious levels of insecurity that create control issues, or is someone who needs to operate with levels of secrecy that confuse the decision making process and interfere with operational effectiveness.

The quality of decision-making is determined by how boundaries are defined and communicated. In a strength-based model, boundaries are clearly defined, everyone knows how far they can go and how to get the resources that they need. "Can't Do" happens when leaders hold people accountable without providing well-defined and consistent boundaries and without giving support and access to the resources needed to do their jobs well.

The following case study demonstrates the power and ability the decision making process to make or break an organization, and the people in it. There were, as you will see, many issues in play. But, at its core, a principal determinant of the organization's demise was the CEO's need to maintain control and to make far too many decisions, no matter how small the detail and how painful to the people around her, leaving little to no room for others to influence or make more effective decisions.

Workin' In the Land of Gotchya: Years ago, I moved to take what promised to be a great senior level position with "an entrepreneurial non-profit" that was completing a turn-around. It was my job as Director of Business Development to build the business base in services and products that supported corporations across the country by helping them to build "healthy workplaces." Sounds great, and it certainly goes with my "Can Do" theme. That said, it was one of the most "Can't Do Workplaces" I have ever encountered. I understood that my job offer came with lots of challenges and "room for growth," so I was prepared to work hard and help complete the turn around, which had been hampered by the economic fallout just after September 11th. However, I knew within weeks of starting that something was not right; it took me a few months longer to figure it out, and a few more months to get a new job and get out. Years later, I continue to be amazed by the levels of unhealthy culture and organizational pain.

The CEO often took a "Can You Guess?" and "No, You Are Wrong" approach to management with all of the staff, but especially with the Senior Managers, of which I was one of three. The lack of freedom to make decisions in the course of doing my job managing people and projects was paralyzing. I shared the spot for third in command and had primary responsibility for bringing in new business. Not much of what I did was right, or so it felt. I was the manager of the grant proposal and reporting process, but not permitted to give direction to the administrative support staff without the CEO's direct involvement. I was forbidden to have non-pre-approved conversations with Board members, two of whom I had known personally for several years, both of whom actively supported my role in the organization to help it move forward. When I asked the CEO for her input in refining the strategic goals while developing the business plan, she responded that she, "did not want to have to bother with that level of detail;" yet, when I presented her with the draft, she was "disappointed" that it was not on target. When we were forced to downsize, I was given two sizable client contracts to manage in spite of my voiced concerns about it hampering my ability to bring in new business, which was my primary role; and then I was "held accountable" in front of the Board for the lack of new business.

Where my part of "Can't Do" comes in is that I took it all very personally and became increasingly angry and defensive, losing my ability to function professionally several times, which really embarrassed me. I had moved 500 miles, uprooting my husband from a job he loved and from a community we both loved to take this job. I had known and interacted in a collegial relationship with the CEO for over a year before accepting the job, including having her invited as a guest and co-presenter at a prestigious national event focused on preventing unhealthy workplace behaviors; and she did the same for me. Our interactions were friendly, open, and focused on innovation and potential for growth for her organization and for the clients it served. So, I was blind-sided and devastated as I discovered the notably sour secret sauce of organizational culture I had been hired into. And very, very angry. At one point, I called one of the organizational consultants who was working with us and spent 10 minutes non-stop venting about how let down and angry I was, so much so I see in retrospect, that I could not hear the coaching and support that she tried to give me. Rather, I just felt more stuck and defeated.

Over the years, I have harvested a collection of important lessons-learned from working in this culture of rigid ambiguity and "gotchya". One is that this kind of negative soup creates a bond among those who survive it. Staff on all levels created a number of workarounds and stealth systems to bypass the boss and her very changeable boundaries and unpredictable moods. When our strategies worked, it was great; when they did not, there was hell to pay. It has occurred to me more than once that we functioned like a group of teenagers, rather than professionals committed to helping others develop healthy workplaces. We would call each other, as teens often do, and say, "You won't believe what just happened!" The sad part was, it was easy to believe what happened. The upside is that as an outgrowth of building our own systems, there remains a very strong bond among the "alumni" that comes from what we refer to as our shared experience of workplace PTSD. I was only there briefly, less than a year many years ago, but I maintain close friendships with two of my former colleagues and social media contact with many of the rest of the people who worked there.

When I interviewed for the position, I had been told that there was a financial reserve that would support the operations of the organization for two years while the transition was completed. It took about four weeks on the job to figure out that was wholly untrue, and that, in fact, there was a significant deficit. Within six months after I left, the organization closed down, which, while not a surprise, was very sad, and again, unnecessary. It was not "all her fault," though that is sometimes a tempting slant for those of us who worked there. But, it was a result of a very poorly designed decision-making model that, over time, alienated staff, Board members and a shrinking number of clients; and, it depleted the organization's revenue to a point of no return.

I have three primary lessons-learned about good decision-making from this situation:

1. Develop a "Can Do" approach to evaluating any job opportunity based on how all four "Can Do" model practices are applied in an organization.

2. When things do start going wrong, do what you can to maintain balance and perspective, no matter how unsettled the situation becomes, so that you are able to make your decisions based on the bigger picture, not just on emotion.

3. Trust your gut about what is going on around you. Know it is okay to leave a situation when your skills, perspectives and contributions, and those of your coworkers, are not respected.

Change & Growth

We all know, and most of us openly agree, that change is hard. Implementing change that is in response to circumstances beyond our control and without the ability to plan is EXTREMELY HARD, yet that is the way change too often happens. The following two case studies, which chronicle my personal experience as an Executive Director during a turbulent multi-year transition period, are offered from my current, much less stressed vantage point of 20/20 hindsight.

More Effective Strategies for Managing Organizational Change: About 15 months after I began serving as the Executive Director of a residential child welfare program, the State, which was the primary funder, initiated a massive change in their system in an effort to move kids out of residential care and back into their communities. At the time I felt that the State did not approach some parts of the change process in the most effective manner and I was also pretty convinced of the need to caringly keep some of the young people in placement outside of their communities. While I still agree with both of those statements, what I have come to realize in the intervening years is that my defensive posture and somewhat righteous approach to the change process too narrowly focused my thinking and actions, and cost me and the agency a great deal of political will and potential funding. Also, what I can see now was my reactive/responsive posture with the State and somewhat top-down approach to working through the huge, multi-year transition with the agency staff cost me even more, and more important, political capital with the people who worked with me. Ultimately, it also weakened and detracted from our ability to help the kids. I attribute part of it to my lack of experience since it was my first job as an Executive Director; and part of it to not listening to my inner "can do" voice and believing I couldn't really know or learn more than the "experts." My posture kept me arguing too long, and learning too little too late.

The net-net of the transition was that while over 75% of our peer agencies closed their doors, our agency did not, so on many levels it was very successful. The agency still remains open and only recently transitioned to a day-school model. But, in retrospect, I see that many of the bumps and unnecessary causalities along the way could have been avoided if "I knew then what I know now." So, I ask myself pretty candidly and share with you, "What could I have done to make it a more 'Can Do' transition process?"

What I Would Have Done Differently #1: I would have made it a much greater personal and professional priority to learn about and better understand the funding and fiscal systems that were critical to operating a multi-million dollar corporation. While I am pretty smart and was well versed in behavioral health and adolescent development, and had a great deal of experience running youth development programs and specifically residential programs, I did not have a strong financial background. As months went by, I learned the financial and accounting ins and outs incrementally and relied on others with stronger business backgrounds to inform and guide the financial decision-making process. This was increasingly risky during the critical first months of the transition, a period during which we lost a lot of money. At the beginning of my time as Executive Director, I pretty much listened to Board members and our CPA or tried to figure the financial reports out myself. I did not ask questions because I did not want to look stupid. Instead, I bought an, "*MBA for Dummies,*" book and read it over and over. Once, as I was beginning to realize that "how much I did not know" was hurting me, I took one of my peer Executives out to lunch so he could explain a concept of the cash flow worksheet that is, in retrospect very basic, to help me settle an ongoing disagreement with the business manager.

As I have progressed from being a first time Executive Director through to being a more "seasoned nonprofit leader", I have discovered that there is a juncture where the larger fiscal strategy meets the budget and program plan that is the dynamic life force of an organization. It is that place where the budget becomes the strategic plan in numbers. I have since made it my priority to understand the location and strength of that sweet spot in every agency I work with, including as a consultant, and to ask as many questions as needed to be sure I see and clearly understand the whole, bigger picture.

My lack of skills and depth of financial understanding allowed other people to shape my thinking on occasions, which sometimes resulted in the negotiations with the state becoming more polarized than they needed to. During the first months of the transition, my lack of knowledge kept me in a responsive, more often a reactive posture to unfolding twists and turns, rather than having a very strong sense of what the impact of some of the State's decisions and my reactions would or could be. By the time I resigned from my Executive Director position, I could wield a spreadsheet and create program models with cost projections with the best of them, skills that have served me well subsequently. I do regret it was a set of skills that I learned pretty late in that very stressful transition, after thousands of dollars had been lost.

If I were writing this as a chapter with recommendations on how best to implement a "Can Do" nonprofit transition, I would restate something very similar to the take away from the first case study: make it your business to know about ALL of the aspects of the Executive's job. That way, you don't over rely on other people to do more than provide you with information to help form your own "Can Do" decisions.

What I Would Have Done Differently #2: I would have engaged staff in the change process very differently. In my defense, it was very difficult in the early months to understand with much clarity what the impact of the changes that the State was making would be, and so I was cautious of sharing too much information, not wanting to create too much anxiety beyond my own office and the Board. The situation was very complex and political, and I was a new and inexperienced Executive Director. To deal with the coming changes "confidentially," I began, with the blessing of the full Board, working with a "steering committee" of six Board members. An unintended consequence was that as I was able to move the agenda ahead with the Board, the managers were left in the dark and this created an information gap that resulted in increasingly negative feelings about being left out. When members of the Board would ask why the managers were not more fully involved, I would respond that until the future of our relationship with the State was clearer, we needed to keep the two processes, running the organization and the changes that were coming, separate. This made sense at the time, but was a critical error on my part.

What I can see, in the 20-20 vision of retrospect, is how that gap and their feelings contributed to the workarounds and resistance that made a very difficult situation even harder. Instead of engaging in dialogues with staff at all levels and laying out the issues and risks to get their input, I conducted briefings with them about decisions already made; decisions where I genuinely, if naively, believed I had fully taken their needs into consideration. And, I might have, but it sure did not feel that way to them! There were many great and gifted staff working at the agency in the years I was there; sadly, I lost a great deal of idea-power by not being more inclusive and respectful of them. There were a number of staff who had a good understanding of and trust in my leadership, and who also understood the need for change. Unfortunately, they often found themselves torn between loyalty to their peers and my agency leadership, which is not a great strategy as a leader to give support to, or get support from, my allies! Then later, when the census was again reduced by the State and additional staffing cuts had to be made, those wounds deepened in painful ways that carried even greater costs.

The highly successful part of the negotiation was the decision to partner with a well-known national organization to adopt their research-based program model, and the State provided a separate grant that paid for the training and the transition. The side-effect of having left the staff out of the lead-up to this great victory was their resistance to adopt the hard-won program model. One of my biggest lessons-learned is that until there is a well-defined staff buy-in in place, the best programs in the world cannot be implemented or sustained.

Another unintended consequence is that some people outside the organization, specifically in various departments of the lead State agency, began to have more influence on the some of the staff than I did. This introduced additional anxiety, as some of the State employees were dealing with their own internal organizational issues related to the State's changing systems. When they shared their perceptions with the staff at my agency, it would sometimes undermine our agency's needs in favor of their own. My staff became more uneasy as time went on, and an unsettled staff does not do a great job of taking care of high-needs youth! So, the staff would act out, and then the kids would act out, which just like in a family system, is one way of communicating that their needs were not being met.

The change-management process that I developed with the Steering Committee of the Board, with its consistent communication flow and incremental strategy-development, was actually an excellent model of collaboration and provided me with healthy, meaningful, and diverse input into a very stressful and protracted negotiation with the State. Every time I heard from the State, I called at least two of the Steering Committee members and discussed what I had learned and its implications with them before responding to my State-employee colleagues about the "issue du jour." I learned so much during those long months of back and forth with the State mirrored by back and forth with the Board members – lessons about strategy and tenacity and positioning. Looking back, I wish I had known to expand that dynamic to include many more players across the entire organization of, at the time, over 120. The staff and managers could have both contributed and learned some of those great lessons, too. We would have been in crisis to be sure, but I think it would have been for a considerably shorter period of time and with many fewer "casualties".

I also realize as I write this, that I did not thank the staff often enough for enduring the stress during the months and months, (and months!), of transition and change. Thank them, not just at the annual awards event or in emails, and not merely another "unhappiness prevention" intervention, but personally and in person with a genuine thank you.

So, if I were writing this as a chapter with recommendations on how best to implement a "Can Do" nonprofit transition, I would boldly articulate:

In preparing for and throughout a change process, it is critical to communicate about the changes – over and over and over again. Use clear and simple language. Don't just dole out information. For major transitions, planned information sessions and updates are recommended, with good follow through for questions raised. Maintain, and then keep, a calendar of scheduled communications, even if there is not much happening because silence when staff expects information creates anxiety…lots of unnecessary anxiety.

Engage employees by asking questions and establishing committees to facilitate the cross agency flow of communication. Get their input and buy-in. When specific changes are not optional, it helps to engage staff by asking not IF, but HOW, something new can be done. Establish boundaries on how information will be provided and clarify up front what is expected from everyone in the organization in terms of confidentiality and civility. It is helpful to keep the organization's values visible and part of the conversation because they provide needed structure and security to help staff participate in healthy growth.

What I Know Now - The two reasons that the agency survived: One reason we survived is, as I indicated above, that we successfully negotiated with the State for a new program model in partnership with a national child welfare organization, and then received support for training and implementation, both time and funds, to implement that model. It was a victory after a huge, hard-won battle that had lasted almost a year, during which time the State would not commit to us whether they would provide this support or not, creating, as I said, a palpable level of anxiety throughout our organization. My mistake was in assuming that once the State's decision to support us was made and the new contract was in place that the remainder of the transition would go easily and smoothly. We had won! Let's all rejoice!

What happened instead was a new kind of unsettledness as the new program model rolled out, and "resistance to change" trumped "the promise of new life." The new program model was very labor intensive, and it only worked if the staff was able to establish solid expectations with the kids. It required extensive training and a parallel effort of: "establishing solid expectations with the staff!" Some of the old staff left, which is not all a bad thing during this kind of transition; but, that left more inexperienced staff dealing with very high-needs kids, which has a major downside. I won't go into detail on the on-going crises and very halting progress, rather I want to focus on what I learned from these painful situations.

One of the things that can be most confusing to a leadership team as it works to sort out and prioritize all of the moving parts of a nonprofit organization is: which are the core, primary drivers of success, and what are the pieces that are important, yet are only responsive to those drivers? What will make things settle down vs. what will move the needle toward results?

Here is the very critical lesson I learned, a bit too late: there are three equally important core drivers in any organization - the finances, the people, and the quality of the program, service, or product. At no time is it more important to keep each and all of those three things in focus than during the very messy, turbulent, and confusing time of an organization's transition. Until there is a well-defined and realistic financial framework in place, the best programs in the world cannot be sustained; if that financial framework does not support excellent programming, it will weaken and fail. And, if you don't have the right people in place who have access to resources and know how to use them, it all will fail!

Mission is the second reason that I believe that the agency was successful. In spite of the numerous strategic blunders and tactical errors that were made, as an organization we were committed to being there for the boys and young men whom others had forgotten and cast aside. We were not willing to give up – during a process that took over three years – until we had a program, financial, and staffing model in place that was sustainable. Sustainable, not for me, not for the staff, not for the Board, but for the boys! The extent and strength of our commitment to the 100 year-old mission gave me the determination and grit to push onward to the next day and take many "one more steps, just one more time" during months of days and nights of confusion, uncertainty and unrelenting crisis. I learned valuable financial, political, and change-management skills as I went – sometimes very unevenly and begrudgingly! These skills could be acquired, but the commitment to mission came from deep inside me. The commitment to mission was what I contributed most as the leader. What I modeled, and what is my legacy to the agency, was my unwavering commitment to mission and to, as we quoted Winston Churchill many times, "Never, never, never give up," because the boys were counting on us when everyone else had let them down.

The Secret Sauce

My Burn Out Made the Sauce More Bitter, Not Better: From the discussion in the case study above on the stressful and lengthy organization-wide transition process at the residential treatment agency, it should come as no surprise that I was totally burned out by the time I made the decision to resign and move on. I had been there just under five years, and over three of those years had been consumed with what I called playing "deal or no deal" with the State on almost a daily basis. That kind of "crisis" management begets additional stresses and drama that can, and sadly did, take on a life of its own. And, during this time, the negotiations with the State were not the only thing keeping me up at night.

While the protracted negotiations and then the transition to the new program model were occurring, we were also taking care of some of the most at-risk, in need, and hurting kids in the state, which is extraordinarily hard work even when there is a four-star "Can Do" organization with lots of money, a great program model and well-trained staff. The kids' histories and stories are filled with years of violence, trauma, and toxic stress. Our residence provided them a much safer living environment; our clinical and behavioral services provided relationships, resources and tools to heal; and our school provided the support, encouragement, and potential for academic remediation and success not available in their local, mostly urban public schools. For many, this was their last chance for healing, learning, and growth before they landed in and out of the criminal justice system for the rest of their lives. They were not an easy group to work with, and presented a series of challenges, that ranged from fighting to running away to hurting themselves, all of which required staff to stay one step ahead at every turn. Given the unsettled environment of those times, there were more than the typical number of "incidents" and accompanying headaches. And, with every "incident" came the risk that it would cause a setback with the State in the negotiations. Several of them did – BIG time.

While all of this was going on at my agency, I was also serving on the Board of Directors of the state nonprofit association which was a player in advocating for the safeguards for the kids and support for the contracted agencies while these major changes were being made to the system.

And, just as the changes coming to the State system were being announced, I was diagnosed with Chronic Lymphocytic Leukemia. Not life-threatening at all, but it did compromise my immune system and lay an extraordinary layer of stress on my psyche and my body.

One of the things that I had to remind myself of over and over again in those years was that this particular change process was totally involuntary, not one that was planned for, or one that challenged our ability to proactively and strategically manage. In fact, we had a strategic plan that continued to get pushed aside because of the State's approach to making its changes and the impact on staffing, finances, and sanity. For example, they would tell us we needed to make further cuts to census and staff, and we would propose a restructured residential staffing model; then it could be three to four months before a decision was made. Once that decision was made on the residential side, we had to make the complementary changes to the school schedule and staffing. These situations made it difficult and awkward for us to cultivate new funders and propose, with any level of confidence, an innovative vocational project or an offsite outreach program.

There was little in the way of balance in the work-life balance picture for me. Work was just about 24/7/365, because the boys were there, yup, 24/7/365. I had an apartment at the agency and stayed there usually two nights a week to get the "regular" work done that was pushed aside during the day while dealing with the negotiation and/or transition. During the months of negotiating with the State for the new contract, when we were technically operating without a contract and at risk of having to close, I was not able to be far from my cell phone and computer to respond to an email or a phone call with a memo or other official reply. I talked with the Board members and our attorney far more than I did my husband. My husband and I went on vacation one March, and I was on the phone or the computer more than I was enjoying the Southern California spring. And, the crisis were not limited to the kids and the transition. I was on a cruise ship in the Caribbean when I got the call that a huge pipe burst in the basement of the 100 year old building, spewing asbestos, (no one had been nearby!), and I was the one person able to authorize the protocols for the HazMat clean up required! One of the kids jumped the fence to the pool in the middle of the night. As we were discussing increased safety strategies, I learned that there had never been an occupancy permit pulled for the pool when it was built, which created a HUGE liability. I needed to shut the pool down for a whole, (hottest), week of the summer while that was being remedied, a move that made me unpopular with just about everyone. And, the list goes on! I was often tired, but I was never bored.

There was a point, in the months before I resigned, that I knew that we had finally arrived at a more secure position with a stronger balance of finances, program model, and people when I began to question whether I was the best person to move it all forward. I was exhausted to my core.

There had been a growing cost to my gradual learning process – to me and to the agency. I was aware that sometimes I fought too hard instead of too smart, and that had, over three years cost me millions of chits in political capital with all of the stakeholders, including the kids. I had started out with, and still had a chip on my shoulder about the whole thing. Some of my indignation was fully and totally righteous, but, as I have since learned, that does not much matter in the scheme of things. And, I was exhausted to the core of my bones. Totally and completely exhausted and burned out. In a "Can Do Workplace," strength-based and servant leadership is a critical ingredient of the secret sauce, and my burning out was part of what contributed to souring it.

My decision to leave was made after my personal, deep reflection on my needs and the agency's needs and many long conversations with my husband. In the end, I knew that the best decision was for me to resign and give a new leader a chance to move the mostly rebuilt agency forward with new energy and less baggage. When I resigned, I gave 90 days' notice to support the Board as they worked on their transition.

As much as I had learned, it took me several more years after I left before I finally "got it!" Got what? Gratitude. That was the critical, but missing element of a "Can Do" perspective in both my personal and professional life. Gratitude is what finally helped me permanently knock the chip off my shoulder and get the "but" out of "yes, but…" As the leader of that organization, I had the mission piece down cold – part of what I lacked were the benefits and resources that are found within a culture of gratitude.

While there were many, many things that happened in those five years that were stressful, painful, and sad, there were many, many others to be grateful for. The State offered us the chance to restructure and paid for the transition and training, and reduced a bit of our deficit to boot! That was HUGE. There were many excellent staff who gave their all to support the kids every day. We achieved a five year certification from the state department of Education and a three year accreditation from the Council on Accreditation. The kids completed elements of their education that had seemed out of reach before, and several attended the high school in the community. I was given a series of unique opportunities to lead, learn, and grow. The Board's commitment to support the mission allowed the agency to survive. That commitment has endured and helped the agency to recently make another significant transition and to attract more funders for sustainability.

During the spring following my departure, I completed an Executive Certificate in Nonprofit Management program at Georgetown University. In the course of the readings, presentations, and discussions that comprise the program, I was able to discover context and systems within which to sort and organize pretty much all of the "school of hard knocks" lessons I had accumulated in the previous five years. My last recommendation is that anyone seriously considering a nonprofit Executive Director or CEO role that does not have an MBA or MPA should experience a nonprofit management or leadership certificate program, if not before, then shortly after arriving. If I knew then what I know now, I would have done that the first year I was Executive Director. It would have been an investment that yielded an excellent ROI!

I have learned so many valuable lessons and had numerous opportunities to use my failures as seeds to my future success, so I want to close with a quote from Arianna Huffington that sums up my personal and professional "Can Do" approach to life.

"We need to accept that we won't always make the right decisions, that we'll screw up royally sometimes -- understanding that failure is not the opposite of success. It's part of success."-Arianna Huffington

CHAPTER 6

"CAN DO WORKPLACES" STRENGTHEN THE NONPROFIT SECTOR

I have a very special place in my heart for the nonprofit sector and the millions of people in the U.S. who work for and volunteer with local, regional, national, and international nonprofits to make a "Can Do" kind of difference in their communities and around the world. With the sea-changes of the last twenty years, and more coming, I believe that we need to strengthen the sector to help nonprofits better safeguard the needs of those whom they serve. This strengthening should not come entirely from the outside, from philanthropists or corporations. Much of this work is ours to do with their support. As long as the funders are doing most of it, I think that the tail is wagging the dog.

▌The Unique Role of Nonprofit Sector

According to the Independent Sector,[xxxvi] over 1.6 million tax-exempt organizations of all kinds (various 501(c) subsectors) were registered with the IRS in 2011. Those with 501(c)(3) classification make up a majority of tax-exempt organizations, numbering close to 1.1 million organizations in 2011. This number includes public charities, private foundations, and religious organizations. What separates a charitable organization from other types of tax-exempt organizations is its purpose: it must benefit the broad public interest, not just the interests of its members. All nonprofits are guided and governed by their mission, a public statement that articulates the single most important thing that an organization does.

In the 21st century, successful nonprofits have evolved to become what Peter Brinkerhoff[xxxvii] calls "mission-based business, not charities. Your organization is in the business of doing mission. Mission first. But a mission-based business acts in a businesslike manner."[xxxviii]

Employees, volunteers, and especially the board members are stewards of the organization and its resources, held in public trust to fulfill their mission, and exempt from paying taxes.

The size of the nonprofit sector makes worthy of attention: According to the Bureau of Labor Statistics, in 2012, nonprofits provided 11.4 million jobs, accounting for 10.3% of the country's private-sector workforce.[xxxix] Between 2000 and 2010, employment in the nonprofit sector grew and estimated 18%, faster than the overall U.S. economy.[xl] The nonprofit sector continued to add jobs throughout the recession and into the recovery.[xli] The nonprofit sector paid $587 billion in wages and benefits to its employees in 2010, accounting for 9.2% of wages paid in the U.S.[xlii] Add to that the role of volunteers in the nonprofit sector: according to the 2013 national data from the Corporation for National and Community Service, 62.6 million Americans volunteered in 2013, contributing 7.7 billion hours of service with an estimated value of $173 billion.[xliii]

Mission is a nonprofits most valuable asset. As Brinckerhoff says in Smart Stewardship for Nonprofits, "The mission is the why of your nonprofit; the reason it exists." [xliv]

Mission goes beyond legal status for tax exemption. The public trust is given to nonprofits because they exist to deliver goods or services for the benefit of the wider community. Brinckerhoff continues, "The ultimate goal for a nonprofit, of course, is better mission for the people you serve."[xlv] When nonprofits keep their mission as the primary and intentional focus they are positioned to stay healthy and grow as "Can Do Workplaces."

First data, then disaster: Sea Change in the 21st Century

Transition to data driven outcomes: In the last 15 years, the nonprofit sector has been transformed by the 21st century "sea changes". Since the dawn of the new century, the nonprofit sector had grown to a new level of prominence, professionalism, and economic influence. Many more resources, financial and human, are being directed toward the sector, evidenced by a swelling of certificate programs and new Masters level programs in nonprofit leadership and management. State associations have grown and new membership organizations have been created to support the work of the "third sector."

"Nonprofit organizations are the cornerstone of our civil society, that network of voluntary associations, individual volunteers, institutional relationships, and social contacts that makes our democracy viable, vibrant, and accountable.

These organizations are perhaps more important today than ever before. They not only supplement the activities of government and business, but also provide the balance that keeps these sectors transparent and in check."

-Pablo Eisenberg, Challenges for Nonprofits and Philanthropy: The Courage to Change. (2005) Medford, MA: Tufts University Press

As a second wave of the Enron fallout of the 1990s, accountability in the nonprofit sector increased, with new scrutiny through revisions to the IRS Form 990 and increased focus on financial transparency, with Board oversight to eliminate conflicts of interest. As a result, Principles and Practices of Nonprofit Excellence were developed and adopted by numerous state associations; and nonprofit risk management guidelines and practices became increasingly required by funders and adopted by organizations. There were also significant shifts from providing loosely defined "programs that help people" to data driven outcomes that measured progress to mission and delivering programs that have with measurable, system wide impact. Nonprofits began to recognize the need to diversify revenue streams for operating budgets and to create and/or diversity the investment portfolios of agency endowments.

The nonprofit sector is at a critical juncture, a time of transition that brings with it interesting dynamics and tensions. On the surface, it appears that the nonprofit sector had started to grow up, face reality, and, (finally, some would argue), become part of the business world. But with these rapid changes and new scrutiny came numerous struggles, challenges, and hurdles. Jim Collins reminds us that it not about the business model as much as it is about developing and sustaining discipline and excellence. [xlvi] The intensified focus on data-driven outcomes and on accountability for the use of funds has presented new and daunting challenges for small and midsized nonprofits, many of whom did not have the capacity to restructure and implement new program models and measure their outcomes to these new requirements.

A core challenge is that funding for nonprofit services and programs has become increasingly competitive. Jim Collins points out in, "***Good to Great and the Social Sectors***," that unlike the business world where profit is an outcome indicator of success, in the nonprofit sector, money, or funding as we call it, is only an input.[xlvii] Funding through individual, foundation and corporate philanthropy and fees for service, usually on a sliding scale, is an absolute necessity to keep the work and the organization going. Philanthropic support is a requirement for nonprofits the same way markets are for businesses.

Where does the funding come from? Private foundations that follow the direction of the interests of their individual trustees. Corporate funders that answer to stockholders. Individual donors who connect with and respond to the mission and work of a particular organization. The result for some nonprofits has been a sad situation of the nonstop, cyclical pursuit of revenue: attracting new funds by trying to match their work to the funders' focus, while trying to keep current funders, and keep them happy with data-based outcomes. Adding to the stress is the situation I have mentioned in other sections of the book: the reluctance of funders to support funding infrastructure, making it difficult to provide professional development to build staff capacity to deliver programs and services to data driven outcomes. It is no wonder that the tenure of more than half of nonprofit Directors of Development is less than two years.[xlviii]

Adding to the challenges above, over the last 30 years, the competition for market share and funding has shifted, and services once predominantly provided by nonprofits are more and more being delivered by the for-profit sector. This trend adds a disconcerting element to the mix and begs the questions: when for profit organizations provide these programs and services, is there the same commitment by individual leaders, managers and staff to the mission and the people being served? Is there a commitment to diversity and building the communities being served from within? In an age when the "economic divide" just keeps getting wider, does this trend somehow contribute to increasing the gap?

The Great Recession: I want to pause here and insert the impact of the Great Recession on nonprofits. While the challenges and changes described above had significant impact on the nonprofit sector, nothing was as significant as the economic collapse during 2008-10, the epicenter of the Great Recession.

While 2008-10 created a turning point and a moment of truth for everyone, many areas of the nonprofit sector were severely impacted. The recession brought a new level of competition for far fewer grant and private donor funds that coincided with a significant increase in the need for services from the hundreds of thousands of individuals served each year by nonprofit agencies and organizations. As a result, many nonprofits were forced to downsize or restructure, cut programs and services and lay off staff.

Funders had never been in such a vulnerable position themselves. While some stepped up to the plate with generous decisions to increase their giving above the standard 5% to help meet the need, I was told personally by dozens of funders during that period that there would be no grants to new applicants, and that they were not sure how they were going to meet the obligations to existing grantees. In the time since then, the sector's recovery has been mixed, just as it has in other areas of the economy. Some nonprofits got very strategic and thrived, like Momentous Institute– some have downsized or restructured and grown, like the Environmental Leadership Program – others merged, and hundreds closed.

The Need to Build "Can Do Workplaces" for Resilience and Results

Nonprofit leader Lester M. Salamon, Director of the Johns Hopkins University Center for Civil Society Studies, is the editor of, "*The State of Nonprofit America,*"[xlix] a seminal publication used as the text for Nonprofit Masters and certificate programs across the country. His perspective on the current state of the sector is a combination of good news/bad news. At a presentation in Atlanta in 2012[l], he discusses, in depth, the extent of the changes and challenges that exist in the sector today, calling this a period of "struggle for the soul of the nonprofit sector." In an article for the Aspen Institute, Salamon concludes, "America's nonprofit organizations, that vast assortment of hospitals and universities, orchestras and opera companies, family service agencies and religious congregations, environmental advocacy and civil rights organizations, soup kitchens, homeless shelters, and more have demonstrated enormous resilience in the face of extraordinary challenges over the past 20 years. As a consequence, this set of organizations has entered the new millennium in surprisingly robust condition, though the re-engineering that has made this possible may be pulling the sector in directions that are highly corrosive of its special character and role."[li] The best of times, the worst of times. Interesting times.

As a "seasoned nonprofit professional," I agree with Salamon, and see the sector as being at a critical juncture of great growth, competing priorities, external pressures, yet in possession of "mission" that is its unique strength within the fabric of the American culture. As nonprofits look toward a future, each and all of the organizations must find the strength and collective will to recognize, advocate for, and expand their role in their communities. Nonprofits need to position themselves, individually and collectively – as an aggregate of over a million organizations with more than 11 million employees and 62 million volunteers – to lead with strength of mission. Defining and providing resources for building "Can Do Workplaces" is my call to action to help them increase their capacity to effectively deal with the challenges, which are not going away, by committing to mission and a strength-based, "Can Do" model. And, it starts, grows, and sustains by building connected relationships between the mission and the people served.

The Benefits & Advantages of a "Can Do Workplace": This book and the "Can Do Workplace" model, with its focus on mission and strengths-based leadership, management, and infrastructure, combine to respond to this need for more courageous mission-driven leadership, one agency, one organization at a time. This book does not contain any major breakthroughs or magic bullets. It is designed as a common sense approach, based on the literature and the experiences of people and organizations that have made it work! As leaders of this sector, we can't wait for others, the funders or especially the for-profit competitors, to take the lead. The risk is too great! The future of the sector rests on the collective strength of the individual organizations.

Instead of being beholden to the funding community, individual nonprofits need to be strong and dynamic enough to join with the funders as full partners in shaping policy and the direction of the sector. Not as co-dependent followers who reshape themselves to meet the needs of the funders, but as the ones who bring the knowledge and expertise for meeting the needs and supporting the successes of those whom they serve. Organizations which, by default, remain "can't do" or "make do", not only risk their futures, they negatively impact the people in greatest need in their communities-and the future of the sector.

Through the "Can Do Workplace," I hope to both issue a challenge to nonprofit leaders to say YES to their missions, the people that they serve, and the innovations and change required to achieve excellence, and provide some of the concepts, tools, and resources to make a "Can Do" difference in their part of the world.

CHAPTER 7

STRATEGIES TO BUILD & STRENGTHEN "CAN DO WORKPLACES"

"Can Do Workplaces" are, by their nature learning organizations, which as we defined from Dr. Senge's work are "…organizations where people continually expand their capacity to create the results they truly desire, where new and expansive patterns of thinking are nurtured, where collective aspiration is set free, and where people are continually learning to see the whole together." To keep an organization learning, "Can Do" leaders create an environment and provide resources, motivation, and rewards for its people's efforts to learn and grow individually.

In a "Can Do Workplace," where innovation is encouraged and mistakes are integrated into a learning culture, providing resources and structured training and learning opportunities is one way to encourage and challenge staff at all levels to engage in learning and value having an opportunity to grow. In his new book, "***The Best Place to Work: The Art and Science of Creating an Extraordinary Workplace***," Ron Friedman quotes Daniel Coyle in his "***The Little Book of Talent***," "Learning and growing on the job is important. When practice is effortless, Coyle argues, learning stops. It's by walking the precipice between your current abilities and the skills just beyond your reach that growth happens."[lii] That said, when you ask employees to stretch, you need to provide the resources to make sure they can be successful.

A pro-active approach to learning & growth communicates that the "Can Do" leaders want their people to succeed, which builds and reinforces the culture of gratitude by allowing staff to feel increasingly valued. According to the work that Robert Emmons did on the importance of gratitude in the workplace, "More people left their last job because they didn't feel valued or appreciated by management than for an improved work-life balance or pay check. Just over two in five (43%) people said that not feeling valued contributed greatly or a fair amount to their decision to leave compared with three in ten (34%) who left searching for a better work-life balance. With the cost of replacing an employee estimated at almost $13,000, consistent, genuine gratitude is a cost-effective policy."[liii]

To support the ongoing leaning process, I suggest several strategies to engage employees and volunteers from across an organization in learning activities that are not that expensive and have the potential for an adding another workplace benefit – fun!

Libraries: Set up a lending library of books and books on CD in a break room and online to promote learning. Be sure to include titles that motivate, inspire and stimulate new kinds of approaches to planning and problem-solving, such as Michael Gelb's "***How to Work Like Leonardo DaVinci***" and "***Innovate like Edison***." In addition to the books and CDs, leaders and managers can develop questions related to some of the books that can be kept in notebooks to help guide the reader to think about key issues specific to your organization. Chapter 8 contains a list of resources that provides a great place to start building a library.

Book Clubs provide an interactive format to generate discussion within teams or across departments on new projects and initiatives, or to generate strategies to address departmental or organizational challenges. The time for the book club meeting should be during the workday, though the reading books or articles can be done during non-work hours. For human services and education organizations, some book club activities can be open to clients and students to increase engagement and provide them with additional resources and support.

Dedicated Meeting Times to Watch and Discuss Webinars, Podcasts, & Ted Talks can provide inspiration or refreshers on key issues and generate new ideas to help achieve goals. The Internet is replete with high quality resources that are free or very reasonably priced. To increase staff buy-in, a small workgroup can be tasked to select the programs or broadcasts, and then calendar the timeslots. And, it is critical that as many of the organization's managers and leaders participate as possible, with emphasis on being a participant in the learning and not to take over the process!

Project-Based Learning: Small, time-limited projects can offer excellent and motivating learning opportunities for new and experienced managers to learn together, as well as providing effective formats for building and strengthening all kinds of teams across and organization. Projects can range from finalizing logistics for the implementation of a new service, to developing materials or curriculum for a new program, or making adaptations for marketing existing services to a new population. For projects that go forward, be sure that the members of that team are part of the presentation. For projects where decisions are made to not go forward, allow a debrief to garner all lessons learned, a process that allows the team to move away from a "failure" label and contribute to the future success of another project.

Team Competition for Innovation in Achieving Goals: Sometimes a little friendly competition will help staff discover a totally new way to move forward on a project or learn about an innovative strategy to launch a service or product. A time-limited competition will produce the most strategic and economical solution. The teams can be comprised of existing work groups or a combination of Board and staff, leadership and managers, volunteers. Be sure to include clients when their input and feedback will add depth, dimension, and effectiveness to a program or services focused outcome.

Getting the Best ROI from Training & Professional Development: In these days when training needs are increasing and training dollars are shrinking, "Can Do Workplaces" employ strategies to make the most out of training dollars spent. Departmental or organization-wide brown bag lunches provide a great venue for the staff who attended a conference or workshop to present a summary of the key takeaways that relate to their work and mission. To increase participation and buy-in, follow the presentation with a brain storming session on how to adopt, adapt, and integrate the best ideas from the presentation into the work or future plans of the organization.

It is also easy and effective to upload Power Point and YouTube presentations from conferences and workshops on the organization's shared drive, and send out a quick email that summarizes the presentation and provides the necessary links to add them to the online library.

Maximize the Potential of the Workplace Environment: The environment and "feel" of a workplace can make an important difference in how people engage, interact, and perform. It is amazing what a fresh coat of paint can do to lift the mood of people in a room, and it is very inexpensive. Ask staff or clients for help to enhance the look and feel of the hallways and program space by using things such as children's art work, and framed quotes with "thank yous" or testimonials from clients or partners, or the organization's mission, vision and values statements. These small items that add warmth and a personal touch will make a "Can Do" difference of their own.

CHAPTER 8

RESEARCH & RESOURCES THAT BUILD & SUPPORT *"CAN DO WORKPLACES"*

Writing this book has provided me with the opportunity, which for me is a luxury, to do research into some fascinating reports and nonprofit and workplace literature; and to read, not just the new publications on the best practices in nonprofit leadership, but to re-read the old standards from Stephen Covey, Peter Drucker, and Jim Collins that have endured the test of time. I also introduced and included related subjects, not always seen as specific to the workplace, such as gratitude. I searched for related ideas on leader- and workplace-focused, as well as popular mainstream daily blogs and websites. This exploration of concepts and resources, along with the dozens of interviews with nonprofit leaders, Board members, and managers from great "Can Do Workplaces" really made my brain hum with new ideas that are connected to or enhance the "Can Do Model." There was so much more related content I could have included, so some of the hardest work was to keep my focus on the elements and practices of the "Can Do" model.

To help you tap into this collection of great ideas and practices, I am including my personal resource list as the final chapter to provide the start of a "Can Do Library". Not all of the resources listed here are quoted in the book, but they have all influenced how I have sorted through the model and what I have written. The list is not exhaustive, rather it is provided as a starting point and resource that can be used in the activities suggested in Chapter 7. Many of these resources provide numerous opportunities to take one step further and use links and references to keep adding new ingredients and some more zest to our secret sauce.

Reports

Gallup Report on the *State of the American Workplace: Employee Engagement Insights for U.S. Business Leaders.* 2013. http://www.gallup.com/services/178514/state-american-workplace.aspx

Institute for Health Care Improvement, *The Breakthrough Series: Institute for Healthcare Improvement's Collaborative Model for Achieving Breakthrough Improvement.* (2003). http://www.ihi.org/resources/Pages/IHI WhitePapers/TheBreakthroughSeriesIHIsCollaborativeModelfor-AchievingBreakthroughImprovement.aspx

Nonprofit HR, *2015 Nonprofit Employment Practices Survey™ Results.* (2015). http://www.nonprofithr.com/wp-content/uploads/2015/02/2015-Nonprofit-Employment-Practices-Survey-Results-1.pdf

Stanford Social Innovation Review, *The Nonprofit Starvation Cycle* by Ann Goggins Gregory & Don Howard, 2009. http://ssir.org/images/articles/2009FA_feature_Gregory_Howard.pdf

World Health Organization *Five Keys to Healthier Workplaces.* http://www.who.int/occupational_health/5keys_healthy_workplaces.pdf

Books on Nonprofits

Brinckerhoff, Peter C., *Mission Based Management – Leading Your Not-For-Profit in the 21ˢᵗ Century*, 3rd edition. (2009). New York: John Wiley & Sons

Collins, Jim, *Good to Great and the Social Sectors: A Monograph to Accompany Good to Great.* (2005). Jim Collins.www.jimcollins.com

Crutchfield, Leslie R. and Grant, Heather McLeod, *Forces for Good: The Six Practices of High-Impact Nonprofits.* (2008). SanFrancisco: Wiley & Sons.

Eisenberg, Pablo, *Challenges for Nonprofits and Philanthropy: The Courage to Change.* (2005). Medford, MA: Tufts University Press

Green, Alison, Hauser, Jerry, *Managing to Change the World: The Nonprofit Manager's Guide to Getting Results.* John Wiley & Sons, Inc. (2012).

Salamon, Lester M., Editor, *The State of Nonprofit America 2nd Edition*, 2012. Washington, DC: Brookings Institute

Books on Leadership

Covey, Stephen R., *Principle-Centered Leadership.* (1990) NY: Simon & Schuster

Friedman, Stewart D., *Total Leadership: Be a Better Leader, Have a Richer Life.* (2008). Cambridge, MA: Harvard Business Press

Gardner, John W., *On Leadership.* (1990). New York: Free Press

Hunter, James C., *The Servant: A Simple Story About the True Essence of Leadership.* Roseville, CA: Prima Publishing

Rath, Tom and Conchie, Barry, *Strengths Based Leadership: Great Leaders, Teams and Why People Follow.* (2008)New York: Gallup Press.

Books on the 21st Century Workplace

Friedman PhD, Ron, *The Best Place to Work: The Art and Science of Creating an Extraordinary Workplace.* (2014)NY: Penguin Publishing

Collins, Jim, *Good To Great.* (2001). NY: Harper Collins

Lencioni, Ted, *Five Dysfunctions of a Team* (2002). San Francisco: Jossey Bass

McChesney, Scott, Covey, Sean, and Huling, Jim. *The Four Disciplines of Execution: Achieving Your Wildly Important Goals* (2012) NY: Free Press

Books That Help Motivate and Innovate

Amabile, Teresa and Kramer, Steven, *The Progress Principle: Using Small Wins to Ignite Joy, Engagement and Creativity at Work.* (2011)Boston, MA: Harvard Business Press.

Andrews, Andy, *The Traveler's Gift: Seven Decisions that Determine Personal Success.* (2002) Nashville, TN: Nelson Books

Covey, Stephen, *Seven Habits of Highly Effective People.* (1989) NYL Simon & Schuster

Dweck, Carol, *Mindset: The New Psychology of Success.* (2006) NY: Random House Publishing Group.

Emmons, Robert A., *Gratitude Works!: A 21-Day Program for Creating Emotional Prosperity.* (2013) San Francisco: Josey Bass

Gelb, Michael, *Work Like Da Vinci: Gaining the Creative Advantage in Your Business and Career* (2006) (audio book by Coach in a Box)

Gelb, Michael J. and Caldicott, Sarah Miller, *Innovate Like Edison: The Five-Step System for Breakthrough Business Success.* (2008) NY: Penguin Press

Heath, Chip and Heath, Dan. *Decisive: How to Make Better Choices in Life and Work.* (2013) NY: Crown Business

Stallard, Michael L. *Fired Up or Burned Out: How to Reignite Your Team's Passion, Creativity, and Productivity.* (2007). Nashville, TN: Thomas Nelson

Blogs

Harvard Business Review: Management Tip of the Day: http://www.harvardbusiness.org/management-tip-day-hbrorg

Seth Godin's Blog: http://sethgodin.typepad.com/

Smart Brief on Leadership: http://www.smartbrief.com/industry/business/leadership

Michael Hyatt's Intentional Leadership Blog: http://michaelhyatt.com/

Ted Talks

Airely, Dan. What Makes Us Feel Good About Our Work? October 2012. https://www.ted.com/talks/dan_ariely_what_makes_us_feel_good_about_our_work

Duckworth, Angela Lee. The Key To Success? Grit. April 2013. https://www.ted.com/talks/angela_lee_duckworth_the_key_to_success_grit

Dweck, Carol. The Power of Believing You Can Improve. November 2014. https://www.ted.com/talks/carol_dweck_the_power_of_believing_that_you_can_improve

Gates, Melinda. What Nonprofits Can Learn from Coca Cola. September 2010. https://www.ted.com/talks/melinda_french_gates_what_nonprofits_can_learn_from_coca_cola

Pallotta, Dan. How We Think About Charity is Dead Wrong. March 2013. https://www.ted.com/talks/dan_pallotta_the_way_we_think_about_charity_is_dead_wrong

Pink, Dan. The Puzzle of Motivation. July 2009 https://www.ted.com/talks/dan_pink_on_motivation

Sinek, Simon. Why Good Leaders Make You Feel Safe. March 2014. https://www.ted.com/talks/simon_sinek_why_good_leaders_make_you_feel_safe

Sinek, Simon. How Great Leaders Inspire Action. September 2009. https://www.ted.com/talks/simon_sinek_how_great_leaders_inspire_action

ACKNOWLEDGEMENTS

I could not have done this project without a number of connected relationships...Some were for an hour, some for a lifetime. This book has its roots in several informal conversations with friends and colleagues shortly after I published my first book, "The Can Do Chronicles," exploring how my "Can Do" approach to my health, life, and financial challenges and creating strategies might connect with and contribute to strengthening the nonprofit organizations and improving their impact for the people they serve. One conversation led to another, then another, and the project continued to grow.

I want to extend my heartfelt special thanks to the people at the four organizations featured in the case stories. They gave me hours of their time, worked with me to probe and test the model and demonstrated that "Can Do" is alive and well in the nonprofit sector:

» Michelle Kinder has been a rock for me and source of wisdom and steadfast support. And then there is the awesome, caring, hardworking staff at Momentous Institute who wake up each morning more committed to changing the odds than ever! I want to especially thank Sandy Nobles, Frankie Perez, Karen Norris, Karla Crowe, Lauren Richard, and Alina Ramirez-Ponce for their time and great insights.

» Dr. Michael Shafer and Evelind Schechter inspire me and it delights me that we have become friends. And I want to thank their committed volunteers from around the world, including Dana and Tim Dunlea, Greg Ruccio and Anne Bannister who animate and share the mission of Warm Heart Worldwide; and to Stan Moore who introduced me to these special people.

» Errol Mazursky, Jenna Ringelheim, and Michael Gagné and the Fellows, especially Kevin Bryan and Mieko Ozeki at the Environmental Leadership Program who believe they can make the world a better place, and they do!

» Yasmina Vinci who inspires me, along with my friends from the National Head Start Association staff, and Head Start Directors, especially Dr. Marvin Hogan and Dr. Tammy Mann, whose steadfast commitment to give every vulnerable child an opportunity to succeed has provided 50 years of opportunity, courage and accomplishment.

An additional thank you goes out to the nonprofit leaders who shared their time, insights, and reflections during the interviews over many months of preparation and research: Lorna Little, Kevin Grunwald, Tom Pié, Rosie Allen-Herring, Robert Sheehan, Frank Juliano, Candida Flores, Scott Shirai, Matthew Moses, Jannah Decanay Maresh, Marcy Rye, and Claire Knowlton.

Kids have always been at the heart of my work. Across many miles and over many years, they are the ones who deepen and sustain my commitment to the work of the nonprofit sector. Thank you to Kim, Dora, Akuah, Emily, Paris, Jenny, Erika, Tricia, Michelle, Trevor, Megan, Drew, Julie, Jamie, Jeff, Joe, Jonathan, Nora, Christoph, Robby, Felix, Jose, Eddie, Sherrie, Michael, and so many more - their stories have become a core part of who I am. I am richer, by far, because of knowing each of these special young people.

And, finally I want to give a special shout out to my husband, Ned Hogan, who has rearranged our personal schedule many times to accommodate phone meetings at odd hours, gone places without me when I needed to just keep writing, and is always there for me in his special, "Can Do" kind of way!

About the Author

For more than 40 years, Cathi has served in local and national youth and family agencies and organizations as a CEO, consultant, counselor, leader, program manager, fundraiser, youth minister, and teacher. Since 2010, she has worked as consultant and writer for numerous organizations, ranging from sole proprietor businesses, to community based nonprofits, to national membership associations from DC to Boston to Dallas to Columbus and many places in-between.

"I relish my writer's role as narrator, story teller and advocate for the mission-based nonprofits and small businesses that are the lifeblood of our communities."

As the CEO of Mount Saint John, Inc. and Girls Incorporated of Worcester, two youth-focused nonprofits in New England, Cathi served as a community leader, collaborator, advocate and fundraiser. She received her Master's Degree in Psychology from Catholic University of America, and a BS in Psychology, cum laude, from the Ohio State University. In 2008, Cathi completed the Nonprofit Management Executive Certificate program at Georgetown University's Center for Public & Nonprofit Leadership in the McCourt School of Public Policy.

In 2013, Ms. Coridan added "author" to her resume when she wrote and self-published, "The Can Do Chronicles," which narrates her journey through health, financial, and personal challenges into a life that is firmly grounded in gratitude and focused on possibilities.

She is an active member of Rotary International, sharing her commitment to "Service Above Self" on a weekly basis with the Rotary Club of Alexandria. Ms. Coridan has previously served on the Board of Directors of the Connecticut Association for Nonprofits, Youth Net (Worcester, MA) and Wilderness Leadership & Learning (DC).

Cathi lives with her husband Ned Hogan and Gracie, their Westie puppy, in suburban Washington, DC, where both are active members of Holy Trinity Catholic Church. They love to travel, primarily on big cruise ships, and have visited Bermuda, New England, Mexico, and many destinations in the Caribbean. Cathi shares her Can Do model and approach to life and work in her weekly blog post (www.candoblog.com) and though a series of podcasts called the Can Do Dialogues. (www.coridanconsulting.com/podcast)

ENDNOTES

i. http://the4disciplinesofexecution.com/

ii. Drucker, Peter. Management Challenges for the 21st Century (1999)

iii. Collins, Jim. Good to Great and the Social Sectors: A Monograph to Accompany Good to Great. 2005

iv. ibid

v. Emmons, Robert A. Gratitude Works!: A 21-Day Program for Creating Emotional Prosperity (2013)

vi. Smith, Jeremy Adam. Five Ways to Cultivate Gratitude at Work. Greater Good Science Center at UC Berkeley. May 16, 2013 http://greatergood.berkeley.edu/article/item/five_ways_to_culti-vate_gratitude_at_work

vii. ibid

viii. Emmons, Robert A. Gratitude Works!: A 21-Day Program for Creating Emotional Prosperity (2013)

ix. Gallup Report on the State of the American Workplace: Employee Engagement Insights for U.S. Business Leaders. 2013. http://www.gallup.com/services/178514/state-american-workplace.aspx

x. ibid

xi. Personal interview with the author

xii. Personal interview with the author

xiii. http://sethgodin.typepad.com/seths_blog/2015/06/new-times-call-for-new-decisions.html

xiv.   Gardner, John W., On Leadership. 1990. NY: Simon and Schuster.

xv.   Dweck, Carol (2006-02-28). Mindset: The New Psychology of Success (p. 48). Random House Publishing Group.

xvi.   Dweck, Carol (2006-02-28). Mindset: The New Psychology of Success (p. 7). Random House Publishing Group.

xvii. Senge, P., Cambron-McCabe, N. Lucas, T., Smith, B., Dutton, J. and Kleiner, A. (2000) Schools That Learn. A Fifth Discipline Fieldbook for Educators, Parents, and Everyone Who Cares About Education, New York: Doubleday/Currency

xviii. Edersheim, Elizabeth. The Definitive Drucker: Challenges For Tomorrow's Executives. McGraw Hill Professional, 2006.

xix.   http://www.ihi.org/resources/Pages/IHIWhitePapers/TheBreakthroughSeriesIHIsCollaborative   ModelforAchievingBreakthroughImprovement.aspx

xx.   https://sites.sas.upenn.edu/duckworth/pages/research

xxi.   http://www.ted.com/speakers/angela_lee_duckworth

xxii. Covey, Stephen, Merrill, A. Roger, and Merrill, Rebecca R. First Things First: To Live, to Love, to Learn, to Leave a Legacy. Simon and Schuster, 1994

xxiii. Dweck, Carol (2006-02-28). Mindset: The New Psychology of Success (p. 67). Random House Publishing Group. Kindle Edition.

xxiv. Personal interview with the author

xxv.   http://www.inc.com/matt-ehrlichman/5-characteristics-of-entrepreneurial-spirit.html

xxvi. ibid

xxvii. Collins, Jim. Good to Great and the Social Sectors: A Monograph to Accompany Good to Great. 2005

xxviii. Friedman PhD, Ron (2014-12-02). The Best Place to Work: The Art and Science of Creating an Extraordinary Workplace (p. 11). Penguin Publishing

xxix. Green, Alison; Hauser, Jerry. Managing to Change the World: The Nonprofit Manager's Guide to Getting Results. John Wiley & Sons, Inc. (2012).

xxx. Gardner, John W., On Leadership. 1990. NY: Simon and Schuster.

xxxi. Gallup Report on the State of the American Workplace: Employee Engagement Insights for U.S. Business Leaders. 2013. http://www.gallup.com/services/178514/state-american-workplace.aspx

xxxii. ibid

xxxiii. http://sethgodin.typepad.com/seths_blog/2015/06/the-tragedy-of-small-expectations.html

xxxiv. Personal interview with the author

xxxv. Personal interview with the author

xxxvi. Independent Sector is the leadership network for nonprofits, foundations, and corporations committed to advancing the common good. The information describing the nonprofit sector was taken from https://www.independentsector.org/scope_of_the_sector

xxxvii. Brinckerhoff, Peter C.: Mission Based Management – Leading Your Not-For-Profit in the 21st Century, 3rd edition. 2009.John Wiley & Sons, NY.

xxxviii. Brinckerhoff, Peter C. (2012-01-27). Smart Stewardship for Nonprofits: Making the Right Decision in Good Times and Bad

xxxix. Bureau of Labor Statistics Commissioner. Announcing New Research Data on Jobs and Pay in the Nonprofit Sector. Bureau of

Labor Statistics, October 17, 2014.

xl.   Roeger, Katie L., Amy S. Blackwood, and Sarah L. Pettijohn. The Nonprofit Almanac 2012. The Urban Institute: 2012.

xli.   Bureau of Labor Statistics Commissioner. Announcing New Research Data on Jobs and Pay in the Nonprofit Sector. Bureau of Labor Statistics, October 17, 2014.

xlii.   Roeger, Katie L., Amy S. Blackwood, and Sarah L. Pettijohn. The Nonprofit Almanac 2012. The Urban Institute: 2012.

xliii. National Data from Corporation for National and Community Service.

xliv.   Brinckerhoff, Peter C. (2012-01-27). Smart Stewardship for Nonprofits: Making the Right Decision in Good Times and Bad

xlv.   ibid

xlvi.   Collins, Jim. Good to Great and the Social Sectors: A Monograph to Accompany Good to Great. 2005

xlvii. ibid

xlviii. http://www.thenonprofittimes.com/news-articles/half-of-all-fundraisers-flee

xlix.   Salamon, Lester M. ed., The State of Nonprofit America, 2nd edition. (2012) Washington, DC: Brookings Institution.

l.   https://www.youtube.com/watch?v=hEwy8KpKHe4

li.   http://www.aspeninstitute.org/policy-work/nonprofit-philanthropy/archives/nonprofit-philanthropy-55

lii.   Friedman PhD, Ron (2014). The Best Place to Work: The Art and Science of Creating an Extraordinary Workplace. Penguin Publishing

liii.   Emmons, Robert A. Gratitude Works!: A 21-Day Program for Creating Emotional Prosperity. 2013.

CPSIA information can be obtained
at www.ICGtesting.com
Printed in the USA
FFOW05n1608231215

9 781628 652345